# CARPEI AUDIENTIAM
## EXECUTIVE LEVEL PRESENCE

Seize Your Audience ✦ Project Competence
Instill Confidence You Can Get the Job Done

# DAN BROOKS

authorHOUSE®

AuthorHouse™
1663 Liberty Drive
Bloomington, IN 47403
www.authorhouse.com
Phone: 1-800-839-8640

Published by AuthorHouse 7/3/2014

ISBN: 978-1-4969-1908-3 (sc)
ISBN: 978-1-4969-1909-0 (hc)
ISBN: 978-1-4969-1907-6 (e)

Library of Congress Control Number: 2014910660

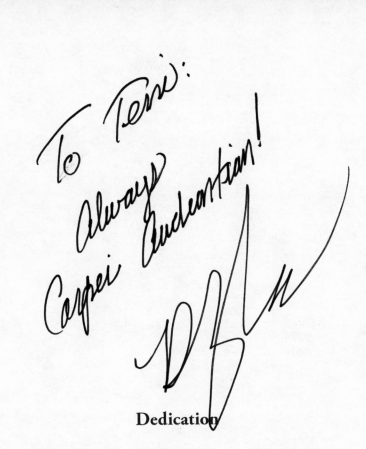

*To Terri:*
*Always*
*Carpei Auditorium!*

## Dedication

For Paul, my brother, who made it all possible.

Repeat these sentences to yourself as you read this book:
"But hey! As you know by now, this is no
big deal. It's only your career."
"And who would *you* want to do business with?"

# CONTENTS

# INTRODUCTION

*You never get a second chance*
*to make a good first impression.—Will Rogers*

It's that critical time in your professional life. You are taking the platform to make a presentation. The audience is composed of ... your critical customers? your internal management?

You've got the classic boardroom setup—the long table in a vertical room. You'll assume the power position right behind the podium, perhaps in the belief that it can be used as some sort of shield if the questioning from the audience gets a little too intense. In your best breaking voice (barely audible above the sidebar discussions, the munching of doughnuts, and the banging of coffee stir sticks against Styrofoam cups), you'll timidly say, "Good morning."

Next on the agenda will be your attempt at humor: a PC joke that you desperately try to tell without offending some subgroup within the corporate culture. Finally, you'll use the laser pointer to deflect all attention away from yourself and over to the screen in the middle of the room. At this point, you could probably put a tape recorder on and slip out the back door and they will never know you left unless someone stays awake enough to ask a question.

Get a grip! These are the critical moments of your career. These are your customers, your critical stakeholders, or God forbid, maybe even your internal management. Are you going to stand up and start like 95 percent of the other speakers with a lousy joke? People are most attentive at the beginning and at the end of your presentation. Why in the world would you wait until the middle of your presentation, when peoples' attention level is the lowest, to make your key points?

This book will talk about how to stand up, seize the audience's attention, set the agenda, display competence, and instill confidence in your ability to get the job done. Who would *you* want to do business with? Fasten your seatbelt, hang on, and get ready to get out of your box, seize the offensive (if you are not ready to do that, don't waste your time reading any further), and at a minimum, go have some fun. Life (even corporate life) is too short not to.

If all this seems like too much muss and fuss for simple meetings, you're probably right. I'm probably overthinking, overanalyzing, and overreacting to the problem. After all, in the final analysis, this is no big deal ... it's only your career.

# Chapter 1

# Executive Summary

*Speeches that are measured by the hour*
*will die with the hour.—Thomas Jefferson*

It's Monday morning, and you're in early because you have that big presentation later this week, and you need to be sure you hit a home run. You turn the corner, step onto the elevator, and right there beside you is—you fill in the blank. Your boss? Your boss's boss? Your CEO? It's the most critical person in the world, the one you need to see in order to get promoted, the Key Decision Maker you have to make an impact on later in the week. The Big Kahuna! The Head Cheese! The Connection! What are you going to say?

"Sure was a nice weekend."

"Wow, these polar vortexes are brutal."

"How are the kids doing?"

"Did your team win or lose?"

Give me a break, folks. If this is a senior businessperson, he or she is in there early for one reason and cares about one thing only: are we making money?

These individuals really don't care which team won or lost over the weekend (and if they really did, they are emotionally over it by now). They really don't care if you know that their kids were away at camp for the weekend. They really don't care where your kids were for the weekend. As a matter of fact, they don't even care whether or not you have kids! What they care about is, are we making money? Specifically, are you making *them* money that will get *them* credit to get *them* promoted to make *them* more money?

What you should care about is positioning yourself to be a critical player in what they care about. Let's say you are on the sales side. Are you going to start with "Hey, I understand it's supposed to be a nice day outside today" when you are going to be stuck inside the office for the next twelve hours? Or would it advance your agenda to say, "Hey, Big Kahuna, I've wanted to have a few minutes to share with you the strategic plan for the sales department this year." You'd then go on to develop your points:

- Our objective is to grow your revenues by 18 percent to $550 million, with a net margin of 22 percent. That means $121 million to the bottom line.
- The key issues that block us from getting there are:
  1. Customers are not aware of the latest upgrades to our product, and
  2. Our biggest competitor will be rolling out a new product in the second quarter
- The focused strategies we are going to implement to overcome those key issues are:
  - A marketing and communications program to existing customers that clearly delineates to them the value proposition for their business in upgrading,

- Targeting of potential new clients that are to be identified by market research, and
- Ghosting the competitor with all our existing and potential customers by showing them how they have so much less experience in implementation of this type of product than we do.

- The critical success factors for us to successfully implement these strategies will be:
  - Consistent field sales follow-up with identified new customer targets, and
  - The refinement and implementation of a clearly compelling value proposition that can be customized to each customer's unique business requirements.
- In order to achieve this, I need your approval of the $23 million budget that we'll be presenting to you next week, which we will utilize to implement our tactical plan.
- All of this represents an ROI to the Company of 7.6:1 for every dollar invested.

There, your executive summary, that will just about take up the elevator ride to your floor. If your CEO or other Key Decision Maker shows any serious interest at all, you might follow it up with, "As a matter of fact, I'd like to get on your calendar to come in and explain in more detail how we are going to execute this plan. Would it be all right if I contact your executive assistant and get twenty minutes later this week?"

As you have undoubtedly experienced in your corporate life, people schedule meetings in one-hour or half-hour blocks, which of course means they back right up into their next one-hour scheduled meeting with zero time to refresh their mind (or body) before the next endless meeting. When I schedule meetings with senior-level executives, I always request just under an hour or half hour. Go for twenty minutes or fifty minutes. If I can't cover it in that amount of time, I can't cover it period! But I have shown the intelligence to realize that the person I'm speaking with would appreciate a break before diving right back into the endless excitement of meetings. And who would you want to do business with?

Of course, as you walk away, the downside of this conversation is that you really don't know what kind of weekend he or his kids had or if his football team won or lost—but do you really care? Especially if you now have the opportunity to come back and lay out the plan in detail? Details are what will get your career noticed.

I'm not saying don't be human, don't show any interest in anything but work. But I am saying that 98 percent of the time, people err too much on having nothing but social discussions. And my life experience is that this is a career-limiting tendency.

You always want to have your executive summary ready to go at a moment's notice. And if you wait until you have to do it, guess what—you'll blow it. So whenever you're walking into the office, you need to be running the little tape recorder (sorry, digital recorder these days) in your brain, going, *What if I bump into so and so?* Whether you are bumping into your customers, critical stakeholders, potential investors, or internal management, you may be called upon to explain what the heck it is you do around here. And you better be able to explain it succinctly.

Have that executive summary ready to go, and be ready to tie it to the bottom line. Make it clear that you are essential to this company achieving its business and financial objectives. When the boss walks away from that elevator conversation, you want him or her thinking, *I wish I had more people around here focused like that who could tell me exactly what they do to contribute to the bottom line.*

Now, if you really want to get out of the box, when you go build your strategic plan, one thing you will do before you put it together is actually read your annual report, or go look at your Web site, or look at your CEO's latest speech. Whatever that individual is doing to position the company, tie your strategy to supporting his or her vision. People might be very prone to argue with you about your executive summary and your strategy, but they will be a lot less likely to argue with the CEO's strategy. Obviously, if you are doing it for a customer, tie it to their strategy. Once again, others may challenge you on your solution, but they are probably going to be a lot less likely to challenge their senior management on the vision that individual has painted for the company. So that none of us forget, let's have the checklist for that Executive Summary:

- *Situational analysis*—where we are today.
- *Objectives*—where we are going (both strategically and financially)
- *Key issues*—those obstacles that prevent us from achieving our objective(s) today
- *Strategies*—the broad strategies that are targeted directly on overcoming our key issues, and how all our supporting tactical implementation plans are lined up to drive those strategies to overcome those key issues
- *Critical success factors*—those key links in the chain that must occur or the train comes off the tracks and we will not make the plan

- *Resources required*—the bucks (or other tangible things) the Big Kahuna is going to have to invest in you to make this plan happen
- *Return on investment*—"This represents a ROI of XX:1 for the company."

You pull that off, folks, and whether it's an internal manager, key customer, or potential investor, you will have that individual thinking, *Wow, that person knows what the heck they're doing and where the heck they're going.* And who would *you* want to do business with, anyway?

Shame on you if you ever walk into an elevator again and have to stand around and talk about the weather because you do not have your executive summary ready to go.

# Chapter 2

# It's All About You: Personal Style

*Speech is the gift of all, but the thought of few.*—*Cato*

Do decision-makers focus on your personal style? You better believe it! You may have the best concept, the best idea in the world, but if you can't stand up and deliver it and instill confidence in your audience that you can make it happen, it doesn't matter. No one will buy. No one will follow. No one will spend their precious time, energy, or resources to support you. You'll go nowhere.

In the end, your audience is asking themselves one question: "Can this person make it happen?" If that individual believes you can drive to success, he or she is going to go with you, no matter what the idea. If the same individual believes you can't drive to success, he or she will not go with you, no matter what the idea.

In the category of projecting competence and instilling confidence, there are four key elements to your personal style: eyes, body, hands (these little suckers will get you in trouble faster than anything else), and voice.

## The Eyes

*The eyes are the window to the soul.*
*—Old English proverb*

The number-one rule of public speaking is to make eye contact before you begin. If you do not have eye contact, the audience is not with you. They're somewhere else. They're disengaged, and you are just creating wind by flapping your gums—and losing credibility in the process. Whatever it takes, whatever you have to do, get eye contact before you go.

My technique is that I will have put my key takeaway, my bottom-line dollar figure of how much this impacts the organization I'm speaking to or my branding up, on a flip chart. I use a few colored markers and a little creative artwork to get my concept up (this means I've gotten to the meeting early), and without any joke, without any "Good morning," and without any "It's nice to see you and thank you for inviting me here today," I'll walk up to that flip chart, smack it in an exaggerated way, and say something like, "Today we are here to talk about how we will implement this program [using the branded name] to drive X dollars to the bottom line."

Ladies and gentlemen, you better believe every head and eye in that room rotates around and goes squarely on you. You have the audience's undivided attention. Whatever it is or however it is you get it, you must make eye contact or your listeners will be distracted and will not hear a thing you say. Stop wasting your time. Do something to make eye contact!

Once you have their attention, begin to look at the audience and focus on individuals. Do not do the classic radar scan with your head flying side to side back and forth across the room—which, of course, is a sign of nervousness. Look at each individual and make eye contact with audience members one at a time. Whether it is an audience of four or four hundred, move your eyes around, making eye contact with individuals. You are not doing this merely to be seen—you are doing this, and this is critically important, to read the audience's eyes and form an opinion of their reaction to your proposition.

By looking in their eyes, you'll be able to tell things like:

- Do they have a concern?
- Are they bought in?
- Are they with me?
- Do they have a question?

You'll even be able to tell if they need that bio-break. You may have heard suggestions to look over their heads or look at the back of the room, but forget that. In corporate America (and this is not true for all cultures), if you don't make contact with the eyes, people believe you are being evasive, are afraid, or do not believe what you are saying. So reach out visually and make eye contact. Read those eyes to know whether they are with you or they have a concern. It is crucial that you form an opinion of where they are.

And by the way, if you don't make eye contact with everyone in the room on a regular basis, those you miss will feel left out and will resent you for it. (*What am I? Not even important enough to be looked at?*) This is how we turn the neutral observers of chapter 9 who want to give you the benefit of the doubt into mortal enemies actively working against you.

Knowing how crucial it is to make eye contact, once you do it, how long do you want to hold that eye contact with an individual? Do you want to make laser contact, stay focused on the same person, move physically closer to him or her, and get into a staring contest? Obviously not.

Instead, you are going to use a technique called STOP—Single Thought: One Person. Hold eye contact for that single thought, read that individual, know if he or she is with you, and then proceed onto the next person. Make that next STOP and then move on to the next person for the next STOP. Single thought, not a sentence and certainly not a paragraph. Just eye contact for a single thought.

Your tendency will be to radar scan because you're nervous, adrenalin is flowing, and your head is all over the place. The audience will immediately interpret this as a sign of nerves, and they'll be right. Slow down! Look people in the eye and read if they are with you, because that is exactly what you need to know.

The worst thing you can do in a meeting or presentation is stand there and, as I like to call it, "show up and throw up." You then walk out of the room with a feeling of relief because it went all right. You make that interpretation because no one else said a thing to object. But we all know what really happens after you leave the room. Your listeners turn to each other and say some version of the following:

- "Well, that sure was a load of crap!"
- "I like the idea, but it's not for us. We might have to change the way we do business and that could be work."
- "Wow, that speaker sure doesn't know us. If he did, he would know that would never work in our culture."

If there are objections, if there are concerns, if there are issues that are going to keep your concept from moving forward, ladies and gentlemen, you want to know about it during the meeting, not after. Later, in chapter 10, we'll talk about how to reach out and process those customer concerns. But at this stage, just read those eyes and know whether they are with you or whether they have a concern.

Another thing speakers typically do is put a PowerPoint slide up, turn, and begin reading off the slide. There are numerous reasons you don't want to turn your back on the audience. For one thing, unless you are blessed with a great posterior, the audience is going to quickly get tried of looking at that view. But even if you do have that great backside, once you turn it toward the audience, your listeners are going to have a tough time hearing you. Your voice is now projecting toward the screen, not toward the audience, and unless you really crank up the volume, you have just changed the dynamics of the meeting and not for the better.

There are a couple of other potential messages you send to the audience when you start reading your slides. Those could be:

1. You don't know your material and therefore have to read it.
2. You don't think the audience knows how to read, and therefore you have to read it to them.

Neither is the message you want to send to your audience. So don't turn your back.

The typical question that comes up here is, "But Dan, I have to see what's on my slide." Well, of course you have to see what's on your slide, but that doesn't mean you read a novel from it. Your slide should be constructed so that the bullets merely trigger what you want to say. Seeing that one or few words should be a sufficient prompt to launch you into your next statement.

You are going to signal the audience when you want their eyes to go to the slide. Let's think about what happens when you turn your head and eyes to take in that next bullet on your slide. As the audience sees you turn your head to glance at your slide, where do their eyes go? To your slide—specifically, the next bullet. When you finish taking in your bullet, after having picked up your trigger for what you will say next, and you turn your head back to reestablish eye contact with the audience, where do the audience's eyes go? They go back to you because merely turning your head back and reestablishing eye contact tells them you are ready to resume. The entire audience now knows what the topic will be from that bullet you all just collectively looked at.

Those bullets are not your entire script. They are merely triggers for what you will say, not the entire printed novel. They are there so that, in the heat of the battle, when you forget what you are going to say, when the pressure is on and you can't remember what it was, all you have to do is pause, turn your head to the slide (as the audience's eyes go to the slide with you), take in the bullet, and think, *Aha! That's what I was going to talk about!* When your head comes back around, the audience comes back to you. One of your key takeaways from this book is to be sure you make that eye contact with the audience. Once again, if you don't make that eye contact, it is considered a sign of weakness. And do people want to trust their future business to weakness?

## The Body

> *The human body was designed to walk, run or stop:*
> *it wasn't built for coasting.—Cullen Hightower*

So there you are on the platform. You're going to project confidence by slowing your eyes down and making eye contact with one person at a time using the STOP technique. But what should your body look like? What should your stance and weighting be?

Well, you don't want it to be the John Wayne Waltz: hands on hips, strolling around the stage, looking at the audience, and saying, "We're going to go make plan this year, pilgrim." That's a little too casual and cocky. On the other hand, you don't want to make it seem that you're running away and hiding behind your podium, flip charts, or anything else on the platform.

You want to come out, stand to one side or the other of the projection screen, and assume the classic sports stance:

- Feet are shoulder-width apart. Why? For balance—so you are not up there on the platform swaying like a tree in the wind.
- Knees are slightly bent. Why? Well, as anybody who has been in the military can tell you, locking those knees will block the blood flow to the lower legs and in about five minutes you will get your audience's attention ... as you pass out on the stage.

From this stance, you are ready to use hand and head gestures to send the audience to the screen for your next bullet. You are ready to move smoothly across the platform and interact with the audience on the other side of the room. You are ready to go palms-up to the audience to ask or acknowledge a question.

When you're standing on one side of the room, the majority of your eye contact should be with those on the other side of the room. While you're physically with one side of the room, you don't want to lose the people on the opposite side. So the majority—but not all—of your eye contact is with that opposite side to make sure you're keeping that portion of the audience engaged and not feeling left out.

As a final point about your body, you want to think about your enthusiasm on the platform. TV commercials make fun of the boring monotone speaker, so you clearly don't want to be that. When you start to see those eyeballs roll back in peoples' heads, think about putting a little more intensity into your presentation.

Now obviously, you don't want to be the cheerleader when you are up on the stage. That is not going to gain you any credibility with Key Decision Makers in the organization. But you do want to have some passion and intensity. Bottom line, you definitely want to punch the key statements that let people know this is where they need to wake up and pay attention. Always remember, if you don't have any enthusiasm about what you're doing, don't expect anybody else to give a rat's rear-end for it either.

## The Hands

*You can pick your friends; you can pick your nose.*
*But you can't pick your friend's nose. -- John Green*

The next element of your personal style is one that will get you in trouble faster than anything else: the good old hands. When you're not using your hands, they should be at your sides. This will feel highly unnatural. But don't worry—if you are like most people, they won't be there long, because pretty soon you will be gesturing.

And it is entirely appropriate to gesture. It's just not appropriate to be the windmill or the landing control officer on the aircraft carrier who is waving the airplane onto the deck. Flailing your arms around like that will quickly wear out the audience and cost you credibility as your listeners begin to realize that there is a tremendous amount of uncontrolled energy racing around the room. It's called a "loose cannon," and nobody, even if he or she supports your idea, wants that rolling around creating havoc in an organization.

When you want the audience's attention directed up to the PowerPoint slide to take in the next bullet, move your hand toward that slide and align it with where you want their eyes (the next bullet point, the bend in the graph, the blemish in the imagery that shows the flaw or disease). When your hand comes back down to your side and you turn your head back to the audience, that is going to tell them that the attention now goes off the slide and back to you. You actually control when and where they look.

When explaining or describing your opinion or vision, it is highly appropriate to use gestures, whether you are going up the mountain, down the river, enacting a golf swing, or whatever it may be. Just don't overdo it, because you will wind up wearing your audience out and leaving them with the impression that while you have a lot of energy, it is probably not all well-controlled.

Now when you are not gesturing, because it's not comfortable to have your hands down at your side, many of us will latch on to something to play with. One of the most common, of course, is the laser pointer. We can use it to deflect virtually all attention off of us and over to the PowerPoint slide. As previously observed, this technique done well can let us hide over at the side of the darkened room, totally detached from the audience and unable to read their eyes.

By the way, has anyone ever seen a person use a laser pointer in moderation? Good golly! People sling that thing around to circle every bullet point on a slide, underline every other word, shakily waver on some arcane number, until our eyeballs are spinning. It begs for some smart ass in the audience to pull one out and start lasing around the room. Dueling laser pointers! Start the banjo music so everyone can forget what you were talking about.

*Lose it!* You are the focus of attention, not your laser pointer. If you can't direct the audience to where you want them on your slide with a gesture and a few words, your slides are too complicated. Your slides—and highlighting them with a laser pointer—are not the value add. You are!

I have a client who recently launched its new corporate training center. I mean the Starship *Enterprise* of training centers. The Ideo conforming chairs. Satellite uplinks. Multiple drop-down or pop-up *laser-proof video screens!* That's right—the laser pointer will not even show up on the screen. Lose it!

Of course, more in the past now are the old mechanical pointers that were used to attack the screen and direct everyone's attention over to it. Then naturally, when we were done pointing, we had to immediately start nervously collapsing and extending the mechanical pointer. It only took a few seconds for the audience to focus on your tick and start counting how many times you were collapsing and extending the pointer. It is an obvious sign of nervousness, and your audience detects it and begins counting immediately. I may not remember a single thing about your presentation, but I can tell everyone, even my wife and kids that night, how many times you collapsed the pointer.

Another famous plaything, of course, is the pen. We stand there nervously clicking it, sounding like we are tapping out Morse code. Or the marker for a whiteboard or flip chart—once we finish writing with the marker we should put it down. But we don't, because then we wouldn't have anything to cling to for security. Instead, we begin twisting it in our hands, hanging on to it for dear life. Then we begin twisting the cap, finally pulling the cap on and off to get the clicks, until ultimately we pull it off and wind up tattooing ourselves on the knuckles, which always makes a great impression with the audience.

Many times we just clasp our hands in front of us in the classic praying position: "Oh God, please let this be over!" That certainly sends a message of power and control to the audience. Or even worse, in the ultimate male-power projection, we clasp our hands over our crotch in the "fig leaf" gesture.

Ahhh … the hand gestures certainly take many forms, not just praying, but sometimes wringing the hands, sometimes just the fingertips of the opposing hands together and pumping them in the famous "spider doing pushups on a mirror" maneuver, sometimes hanging on to a ring because of the nervous energy, the excitement, and the pressure we feel.

I have observed that women often will carry a notepad to the platform with them and hold it to their chest with their arms crossed—apparently holding on to this shield as if, in the event the questioning gets a little too intense, they can slink down behind it and use it to deflect the tough questions. Once a woman has assumed this defensive posture, usually the next thing to come along is the hair flicks. Her hair is out of place or hanging in front of her eyes, and she begins attempting to flick it back into position. Then jerks like me in the audience begin counting *three … four … five.* Needless to say, I have not a clue what she's talking about. I'm busy counting the hair flicks.

So ladies, be sure to groom your hair in a fashion that will not tempt you to be up there doing the hair flicks in front of the audience. When the heat is on, nervousness sets in.

If we have managed to only use appropriate gestures and keep all the playthings out of our hands, we still can't get the hands down at the side. Before we do that, we'll have to go into what we call "anatomical mining." Now, 95 percent of the time, when a man takes a platform, where do his hands go? You got it—right in the old pockets. Of course, he begins playing with all the change that's in the pocket.

When I was a young boy growing up, I'd go to church with my father. He was one of the most articulate people I knew in the world. He was very active in the church and was often called upon to deliver a prayer during the Sunday-morning service. Dad would stand up and his hands would go in his pockets, and I never heard a prayer that man said. I was constantly trying to figure out what tune was being played with the change in the pocket. "Brown-Eyed Girl"? "You Ain't Nothin' But a Hound Dog"?

For men, the first rule is, don't put your hands in your pockets. But if you violate that rule, don't violate this one: get all the change (and everything else for you to play with) out of your pockets. Get that on your checklist before you ever take the platform.

Even if we thought well ahead and took everything out of our pockets, now we put our hands in our pockets and start nervously moving them around inside. Pretty soon, the audience is wondering if we are nervous or are just playing pocket pool. Either way, the audience picks up on it and begins smiling and chuckling. As the presenter, we of course are looking to engage the audience and read their eyes, and we immediately begin to smile and chuckle and think, *Hey, I'm connecting with these people—they're with me—I'm getting through to them.* About now, the audience is trying to figure out what are we playing with in our pockets that is causing us to smile and chuckle. And whatever someone might say, they are all thinking this guy is having way too much fun with his hands in his pockets.

So gents, get those hands out of the pockets. Indeed, I know some speakers who, in order to avoid this, will actually use the hotel sewing kit to put a stitch in place to keep their pockets closed on their trousers and remove all temptation.

Now, once we do get our hands out of our pockets, we still can't keep them down at our sides. We still have an overwhelming urge to *do something* with them. I have seen people begin to play with their posteriors. (It appears that day their underwear just went the wrong way and they have to dig into the situation to straighten it out.) I have also seen speakers let their little pinkies drift up the side of their heads and begin clawing about in their ears, not even realizing that they are hauling out ear wax in front of either their critical management or their customers.

And, yes, for some months now one of my partners and I have been debating about a speaker who let a finger drift up toward the nasal area—and just as in a *Seinfeld* episode, left the audience with that lingering question: was there penetration? And don't you want to rush up and shake that person's hand when he comes off the platform? So, once again, when you're not gesturing, get those hands down to your sides, because those little suckers will get you in trouble faster than anything else.

Now, there is one other big no-no for the hands when we are on the platform: pointing into the audience. If you don't believe this, just try it next time you are on a platform giving a presentation. Even if you were going to that person in what you thought was a nice way, by pointing you have put him or her on the spot. The entire room is now zeroed in on this individual because you have gone right at him or her with an aggressive move.

Pointing is highly aggressive in our society. After all, when do we use it most? When we are lecturing our kids or anyone else for that matter. (Remember the famous finger-wagging and "I did not have sexual relations with that woman!") And is that really how we want to make our audience feel?

So no pointing! Even if you intended it as a joke or to single someone out for a positive reason, it is highly aggressive and will be interpreted as such by the audience. They will be thinking to themselves, *This clown could be singling me out next!* There's no quicker way to flip an audience from wanting to work with you to becoming highly defensive and reserved.

Instead of pointing when you want to engage the audience, you want to go palms-up and move slowly toward the person. Whether you're looking for support or responding to a challenge (see chapter 9), go palms-up and move slowly toward your questioner or the person you want to engage. It will show strength. It will show confidence. And it will show that you can engage proactively in a nonaggressive manner.

## The Voice

*The voice is the second face.—Gerard Bower*

When you think of great voices, whose comes to mind? When I hear James Earl Jones say, "This is CNN," well, that's a fact, Jack. Oh, if we could only get the gravel he has in his voice into ours! For females, I think Oprah has a wonderful, controlled voice. She has the ability to start you off, take you up to the heights of ecstasy, plunge you down to the depths of depression, and bring you right back to reality, all in the space of about forty-five seconds.

Obviously, not all of us are blessed with voices like these talented individuals, which means we have to be even more cognizant of how we use our voice when we're in front of Key Decision Makers.

The biggest mistake is not speaking loud enough. Look at the size of the typical meeting room. Even if it's a conference room, there is still a lot of space in there, the air-conditioner is blowing, the projector is blasting hot exhaust, and people are flipping through our presentation, stirring coffee, and munching doughnuts. Yet most of us will take the platform and begin speaking in a normal conversational tone.

You'd better ramp it up if you want to compete with all this extraneous noise, especially if it's after lunch. If you are doing a good job of making eye contact and reading the audience, you'll be able to tell if your voice level is right. If the audience in the back is leaning forward, if heads are tilting to one side a little bit, your volume is too low. Likewise, if the people in the front row have a "deer in the headlights" look and are leaning back in their seats and seeking to push away, you might be coming on just a little bit strong.

The rule of thumb whenever you take the platform is to take it up two notches over what would be your normal conversational tone. And, again, by reading the audience, you will be able to tell if your voice is at the right level. Why do you want to be sure it is strong? Our society equates a strong voice with conviction in your beliefs and a weak voice with lack of conviction and lack of willingness to battle, claw, and fight for your position. So when you take the platform, go up there and crank the voice up. Read the audience, adjust as needed, and you'll come across as clear and confident.

If you are speaking to a larger group, you may have to use a wireless mic. (I know you wouldn't even be reading this book if you thought for a moment you should stand at a podium and use the microphone there.) We have all seen what happens next—when someone gets introduced, they take the platform, the mic is passed from one person to another, and the speaker then has to clip the mike onto a collar or lapel and say, "Test. Test. Can you hear me okay?" Pretty powerful way to start your presentation, right?

How can you avoid this less-than-inspiring beginning? Well, you're going to get to the room early, well before your scheduled presentation time, and manage the acoustics. Get the wireless mic, put it on, do a sound check, and adjust the volume to where you want it. Of course, you're going to say, "Well, other people will be using it before me, and they will mess up my setting." That is why you will carry a small marker pen with you and mark your spot on the volume knob. That way, when you do go up and someone hands you the mic, all you have to do is clip it on and adjust the volume knob to your mark, and you are ready to go at the right volume. You can launch right into your high-impact opening statement.

Another critical consideration with the voice is pace. It's closely related to intensity and enthusiasm—and just as with intensity and enthusiasm, we do not want to be wearing the crowd out by going too heavy, and we sure don't want to be putting them to sleep by going too soft. If you happen to remember the old Federal Express commercials where the guy would come out talking a mile a minute, and while you knew this person had something to say and someplace to go and a lot of activity to get done, you got worn out just listening to him.

Keep your own pace "business reasonable." When you do come to your critical points and key takeaways, the vital things you want the audience to remember, absolutely pick up the pace and put on some emphasis so the audience knows to pay more attention at this time and remember it in the future.

One of the biggest problems we all have with voice is those connectors—the aahs, the umms, the ands, the nervous tics, or the clearing of the throat. We all know how distracting these can be. You pick up a nervous connector, "Exactly," and just like having a plaything in your hands, if it is bad enough, pretty soon the audience is focused on counting the number of times the connector "Exactly" occurs and forgets all about your message.

When do connectors occur? When we are searching for our next words. We finish our statement, we try to think of what we want to say next, and because we are take-charge people, because we are in control, and because we cannot stand for silence to exist, we will immediately fill it with "ahh" or "umm" or "exactly."

In a formal presentation, this occurs most frequently when we have finished talking about one of the bullets on our slide, and we turn our head to take in the next bullet. Rather than let our head turn or hand gesture direct the audience to the next bullet, we have to put in the "ahh" or the "and," because we cannot stand for the silence to exist. If you don't think you do this, just ask a close confidant to observe your next presentation and provide you with the unvarnished truth.

No, *exactly* is not a misprint. It's just the latest connector I observed in a meeting. The presenter's response to everything was a connector. "Exactly!

If connectors do exist for us, how do we get rid of them? There are two techniques. The first is more difficult than the second. In the first method, you have to train yourself that whenever you finish speaking, you park the tip of your tongue between your front teeth. Now, you don't want your tongue sticking out at the audience, and you don't want to be so tense that you are biting half of it off. But if you put the tip of your tongue between your teeth (actually just push it up against the back of the front teeth), you cannot say a connector. So, train yourself—whenever you cease talking and turn your head to go to that slide to take in the next bullet point, park the tip of your tongue between your teeth.

Now, as I stated, that method takes a lot of discipline. You want the easy way to curb the connectors? Well, if you've got kids or nieces or nephews, all you have to do is get in front of them and ask them to listen to your talk. Tell them it doesn't matter if they understand anything about what you're saying, all you want them to do is yell out every time you say "ahhh" or "umm" or whatever your connector is.

Two things will occur. In about five minutes, you'll want to kill your kids (or nieces and nephews). In about eight minutes, you will be cured of your connectors. If you don't want to subject yourself to that harassment, you will never get better. As adults, we are so hardwired at this stage of our lives that if we don't

- actively want to change,
- engage in proactive behavior to change, and
- have that new behavior continuously reinforced until it becomes habit
- then we will never change. Lose those connectors!

One time I was conducting a program where a lady had a name spelled a certain way on her name tent, but it was actually pronounced another way. At lunchtime on the first day of the course, the person who was the Key Decision Maker for the customer who had bought the course said, "It is going great, Dan, and my people are getting a lot out of it. But you have mispronounced *her* name several times. She's gotten her feelings hurt about it, so from now on, please remember to pronounce her name correctly."

Well, of course I knew that in the heat of the battle, with the audience focused on me, with me trying to process what I was saying later on, I would look at that name tent and revert back to pronouncing her name the way it "looked" to me. So when we came back from lunch, I started off the afternoon by acknowledging to the group that I had mispronounced her name, and I apologized for it. I then asked the group to help me out, saying, "Every time I pronounce her name wrong from here on, would you please heckle me?" They heckled me twice, and I was cured. But if I had never had the audience heckle me, I would have continued pronouncing her name incorrectly to this day.

Bottom line is, whether you do it with your children or whether you use colleagues you have a comfortable relationship with, you've got to get help on those connectors or you'll keep them for eternity.

I often observe that when the audience engages with questions, the connector for the speaker becomes "That's a good question." Every time someone asks a question, the speaker says, "That's a good question." And that continues until one time you forget to say "That's a good question," and now you have a person sitting there with hurt feelings because everyone else got a "That's a good question" and he or she didn't.

Worse, someone asks a stupid question, and you use your connector to say "That's a good question." Now the audience members are saying to themselves, *Is this person really that stupid? He thought that was a good question?*

At one point in my career, I was working for a Fortune 500 IT company and sitting in on a presentation that was being given to the COO. We'll call him John. John asked a question, and the presenter said, "That's a good question." And before he could go any further, John said, "I really don't care if you think it's a good question or not. I want to know the answer." Don't pass judgment on the question. Just answer it.

## ...And a few other things you must manage successfully

## Going to the Audience

Before we finish up with personal style, I want you to remember one key takeaway: when in doubt, go to the audience. When you're on that platform, when you're on the stage and the heat is on and you don't know whether the audience is with you, drifting, dazed, confused, or just doesn't care, go to the audience.

If you can't tell if your topic is relevant to the audience, don't stand there and wonder or proceed on with another forty-five minutes of blathering. Ask, "Is this relevant to you?" Because you are a lot better off knowing sooner rather than later. Read those eyes! If you look at a

Key Decision Maker and you think he or she has a question, ask! Try something like the following:

- "Looks like you have a question about this?"
- "This seems to be resonating well with you. Are we hitting the mark?"

The key is to take control and proactively engage the audience, not wait for them to ask you questions. I tend to check in with the audience at each key point I want to make in my presentation. I check in with the Key Decision Makers and confirm whether this is making sense, they are bought in, and we are good to proceed to the next key point.

If I should get asked a question and I'm not sure of the answer (or even if I am, but I want time to think and frame my response), again, I go to the audience: "Audience, did everyone hear the question? What do you think?"

In this way, I get input from the participants (and if they are engaged and interested in your subject, I promise you they want to speak and provide their opinion). At the same time, I have bought myself time to think about my response. Let the audience members speak. Listen to their opinions. I often pick up additional ideas that I would not have come up with on my own.

I now take any good ideas I've picked up from the audience (I do not use the bad or less than intelligent ideas), take time to think about comments I would have added myself, and then provide that as a more comprehensive answer. Obviously, if that answer reinforces comments that Key Decision Makers in the audience themselves have made, well, that's how I gain their buy-in. (How do you feel when someone in front of a room states to the group that you had a good observation or thought process?) Adding any additional value with my original thought and comments then positions me as endorsing what the audience has said is good and highlighting value even beyond what they saw. I am positioning myself as an advanced or strategic thinker ... and who would *you* want to do business with?

*Remember, read the eyes, and you'll know when to ask a question!*

## Humor

Another important part of personal style is humor. Where and when should you use humor in your presentation? Well, first, let's talk about where you should not.

In your life experience, how do most presentations or speeches in corporate America start? Usually with a joke. Oftentimes a bad one. But a joke nonetheless. Research tells us we have the audience's maximum attention at two points during our presentation: the beginning and the end. Do you really want to spend this critically important time delivering a joke? Do you want to start the usual and customary way everyone else starts a presentation?

Obviously not! I don't want mine to be just like the hundreds of thousands or even millions of speeches delivered every year in the corporate world. As previously discussed, I am going to take these critical times, the beginning and the end, to get out my high-impact value proposition for the audience—a statement that grabs the audience's attention and translates to their bottom line and why it is in their interest to be here and participate in this business discussion.

But certainly, it is okay to inject some humor in your message. Indeed, if you're particularly powerful on the platform, it can be nice to work in some good-natured humor poking a little fun at yourself to show you're human and do not intend to project that you are in any way above or superior to the audience. At the same time, we have all seen a presentation where someone stands up and on every PowerPoint slide is either the *Dilbert* or *The Far Side* cartoon. Now, I love a good joke as well as the next person, but after the first couple of slides, I figure it out. And after the third slide, I'm beginning to ask myself, "Are we here to discuss our critical business issues or read comic strips?"

So the bottom line on humor is like anything else in your presentation: *as soon as anything becomes predictable, lose it!* If every time you throw up a slide you have a joke, lose it. If every time you throw up a slide you start off with, "And let me tell you," lose it.

Why do you want to lose it? Because you want to be unpredictable when you are on the platform. You want to keep your listeners on their toes. They don't know what you might do. You might call on them and ask them a question next. They better be paying attention. So, not only for your humor but for anything else on the platform, be unpredictable. Keep the audience off guard, and you'll retain more control. There's an old adage, "The best defense is a good offense." Go on the offensive!

Having said all this, I can't resist telling a story about one time when I heard an executive from Japan take the platform to speak to a predominantly American audience. He pointed out that in US corporate culture, most speeches start with a joke. In Asian cultures, to show the speaker's humility and desire to connect with the audience, most speeches start with an apology. So he started off his speech by pointing out these two facts and then saying, "So today, I apologize, that I have no joke for you." Blending the two cultures, I thought, was pretty clever. It certainly was different.

## Choosing Your Words

And now, a word about words when you are on the platform: *No soft words* in your presentations. Lose terms like "I would like," "I hope," and "I think."

Remember that John guy I was talking about a few pages earlier? You know, the COO at the Fortune 500 company. Well, I was presenting our proposal that was about to be submitted for a major hundreds-of-millions-of-dollars competition. The bid and proposal budget (money the company spent merely to have a proposal in the competition) had been $1.75 million. As I was wrapping up my presentation I said, "And John, I hope the customer is really going to like this one."

John (who I did learn a lot from, although I don't think we'll ever be drinking buddies or exchange Christmas cards) leaned forward in his chair and said, "You hope? What are we supposed to do now, Dan, get rosaries out and start praying? Please tell me you have something more than 'hope' after spending one and three quarter million dollars!"

Soft words are like blood in the water to management sharks, who start circling for the feeding frenzy fast. I quickly learned to get rid of those soft words.

I should have said: "And John, by selecting our proposal, the customer will indeed be implementing their own strategy since that is precisely how we aligned our value proposition: to enable them to successfully implement their own strategies."

Here's how you can substitute more robust language for those soft terms:

- Instead of "I would like ..." try "This will drive ..."
- Instead of "I think ..." try "Research tells us ..."
- Instead of "I hope ..." try "We have aligned the selection and implementation of our proposal to support the customer's strategy of ..."
- Instead of "We kind of ..." try "We are implementing ..."

You get the picture. Action verbs. No soft words. Strong words show you're going to *go* someplace; you're not just going to drift there.

We most certainly cannot control all factors, but those we can we want to be darn sure we leverage to the max. And who would *you* want to do business with?

## The Right Amount of Nervous

Now, when you take the platform, you're going to fall into one of two categories. The overwhelming majority of us will be in the category of "too nervous." What can you do about being too nervous when you take the platform? First off, apply a little common sense and don't drink sixteen cups of super-caffeinated espresso that morning just before you take the platform. If you've got too much nervous energy and are afraid you're going to be tap-dancing on the stage or talking too fast, take a walk just before you go onstage. I even know speakers who will do some isometrics before they take the platform—just pushing against the wall or chair to release some of that nervous energy and bring it down a notch.

When I'm feeling nervous, I run through my mind the worst-case scenario. What's the worse thing that can happen to me on a platform? Well, in the worst case, the audience would go, "Dan, this is a lot of crap, and don't ever come back in here and waste our time again with this stuff." Now, I don't want that to happen, and I'm going to do everything I can to keep that from happening, but if that's just the case—the audience members say my topic has no relevance to us and why are we wasting our time here—well, folks, frankly, I've got other clients I can call on. I do have my health. I've got five beautiful kids and a lovely wife that I'll be having dinner with or go hiking with this weekend, the dog will still be thrilled to see me when I get home tonight, and there is only so much you can do to me. Even if you throw me out of here, I'll still have other clients to deal with, the sun will come up tomorrow, and I will survive. There's only so much you can do to me. (Of course, it's easier to survive a bad external meeting than a bad internal one, so plan and practice accordingly.)

Now, for that smaller percentage who may think they are really good on the platform, the danger is getting *too* relaxed. It usually comes off that way, anyway. You get on the stage and stroll around like John Wayne, lean up against the podium, begin speaking real casual, and use the laser pointer to generally direct people back over to the PowerPoint slides. You bask in pontificating about your superior knowledge. Ladies and gentlemen, that's way too casual, and it comes across to the audience precisely that way—so much so that they begin to wonder if you have enough respect for the time that they are taking out of their busy schedules to listen to you yammer on. There is nothing casual about this. Your livelihood is at stake, as are their critical business issues. Otherwise, you're not talking about the right things.

The ideal way to feel when you take the platform is "a little nervous." When I'm a little nervous, the adrenalin is pumping; my eyes are sharper and taking in more information; my brain is processing faster; all my senses are heightened; frankly, the air is a little sweeter. It's good to be a little nervous. Indeed, when I take the platform, if the hair on the back of my neck isn't standing up, I get concerned that I have really taken this too casually. Just when I'm most comfortable in the saddle is when I'm most likely to get blown out of it. Being a little nervous is a good thing.

In summary, on your personal style, avoid these common mistakes:

- not making the right eye contact (either avoiding it or doing the rapid radar scan)
- overuse of connectors
- pacing the stage

- not knowing what to do with your hands
- relying on soft words
- doing anything that prevents you from using that stage to take control and exert platform power

Never forget, your personal style plus the power of the platform equals your greatest asset. Use it. It will set you apart from the 90-plus percent of people who do not. And who would *you* want to do business with? In the end, it's all about you. Your listeners—whether internal or external customers—are asking themselves, can you make it happen?

# CHAPTER 3

# COMING ATTRACTIONS: POWER INTRODUCTIONS

*Be yourself; everyone else is already taken. – Oscar Wilde*

We all make introductions all the time, whether formal ones for business or just everyday social and casual ones. The question for the business environment is, do you make good introductions? And really, the more important question is, do other people make good introductions for you?

Power intros are so important that the one thing we're not going to do is leave it to chance. Let's try a little exercise. Imagine that you're about to be introduced to the most influential group in your professional area. These people have the power to make or break your future. Now take a piece of paper and list the highlights of your career, all those reasons that make you uniquely qualified to be speaking to this group on a certain subject. You should include key career achievements, any publications you may have done that are relevant to the subject, number of years of experience, a synopsis of your educational background—anything that would say specifically to that audience why they should be paying attention to you.

Now envision yourself standing up and using that piece of paper to introduce yourself to the group. Obviously, most of us would feel very uncomfortable, and people sitting in the group would probably look around and mumble to themselves and their colleagues, "Wow, what a pompous ass! He sure does think a lot of himself."

Indeed, most of us are very uncomfortable about telling an audience how brilliant we are or how our life experiences are important enough for them to learn from. So what do we do? We can't stand up and deliver this glowing summation of our own career, lest we be seen as egotistical. But how do we convey to the audience what our strengths and accomplishments in this field truly are?

Well, the answer is pretty simple, folks. To be power-introduced to a group, get the Key Decision Maker of that group to do it for you. This group of customers or internal managers might be slightly prone to blow you off, but if their boss stands up and says how important it is that they listen to you, they are a lot more likely to pay close attention.

But you cannot just forward your résumé along to this person and hope that he or she gets it right. We all know what will happen with that setup. Five minutes before it is time to introduce you, the person will, for the first time, look at the résumé. He or she will then proceed to stand up and start reading from it. Wow, it really shows that this person knows you well and has a close association, doesn't it?

Prior to the event, you have to take your résumé and condense it down to a few bullet points, making it clear why you are uniquely qualified to be speaking to this group. I even put it in a bold, sixteen-point font on a sheet of paper for the Key Decision Maker who will power-intro me and make darn sure I get it to him or her days in advance, with an accompanying e-mail suggesting that if he or she wants a little data on my background to introduce me to the group, here it is.

In addition to the actual script of my power intro, I include a second sheet—a PowerPoint slide that is a bulleted, abbreviated version of the first sheet. After reading the actual script, the person doing the power intro can utilize the PowerPoint for the actual introduction. Just like the bullets on our PowerPoint slides, this will trigger the person to state the words without having to dryly read the page. Less reading plus more eye contact with the audience equals more impact.

Here's the format you need to follow to make these power intros work. Start with an opening statement that positions you as an authority on the subject: "Our presenter today first learned the importance of [your area of expertise] as a [your relevant life experience that the audience can relate to] over the past [years of experience]." Continue with a mention of any life experiences that make you uniquely qualified to be here (and hence why the audience should pay attention to you). Include a reference to any relevant awards, recognitions, or publications. Add a description of your education if it is complimentary or unique to your topic.

As a final touch, add a little humor about yourself in your power intro that only someone who is close to you would know. For instance, in my power intro, I wrote, "He holds an MBA from the Florida Institute of Technology and a bachelor's in economics from VMI. Now, many of you may think that stands for Virginia Military Institute, but if you talk to Dan's wife or his children, they will tell you that it really stands for 'Virginal Mental Institute.'"

So everyone has a little chuckle. But think about the subtle message. Here is the audience's boss sharing some personal humor about you. The message that just went to this audience was that their boss really does know you personally. Once again, while that audience might have a tendency to blow you off, chances are they're not going to blow their boss off when he or she gets finished telling them how important you are and demonstrates personal knowledge.

To add some final dramatic flair, the last bullet point on your intro should be, "Ladies and gentlemen, it is my distinct pleasure to introduce [fill in your name]." Withholding your name until the end of the introduction creates a little suspense for the audience, and that is a good thing.

Now I know what you are already thinking: *"Dan, I can't be so brash as to ask a high-level Key Decision Maker who I don't even know to provide my introduction."* No? Let's think about it. When an e-mail requesting the power intro shows up, logic and experience tells me people on the receiving end will have one of two reactions:

- Having already been aware of this technique, they immediately recognize they are dealing with another professional who routinely speaks. I believe that elevates my stature.

- Not being familiar with the technique (and I find that, shockingly, this is true of about 75 to 80 percent of Key Decision Makers), they are happy to pick up a valuable business process, one that, if they are a senior-level executives, they need to know. After all, don't most C-suite executives seek to speak publicly to get their company's message out? Even if they don't ultimately deliver the power intro, you have brought them a valuable business tip. I have found there are few faster ways to establish my credibility and value than by helping someone's career.

Now, we all know it's not a perfect world, and I can't guarantee that the person you ask will power-intro you; but I know one way to guarantee that it will never happen is to never ask in the first place. So let's all agree to try and that our first option will be to go as high as we can. The highest-ranking person attending the meeting is going to be our first option, and shame on us if we do not attempt that every time we are going to be speaking.

But if we simply cannot get *the* Key Decision Maker, let's get the highest decision-maker within that organization that we can. If you can't get anyone in that organization (and I mean you really, really did try), you drag along one of your business associates to deliver the power intro. Really, anyone can do it, as long as it is not you. That way, it will not sound like bragging but will position you as a unique authority on your subject.

Of course, among you die-hards, there is still some Doubting Thomas out there who will say, "Well, Dan, I can't always go to the time and expense of having an additional person travel with me to all my engagements to power-introduce me. And I have tried and can't get any customer on the face of this planet (or within the relevant company) to do my power intro."

All right. All right. If you can't get beyond asking a customer to introduce you, and no one from your team can go with you, and in the end you are stuck with yourself, stand up and power-intro your organization:

- Explain what makes your organization an authority on the subject.
- State its number of years of experience in this field.
- Add, "If you want to know more about me, my CV is in the back of your handouts ... knock yourself out."

Obviously, this is where you have your bulleted, high-impact statement of why you are a unique authority to be speaking to this group. (I really don't even like suggesting this as an option, because it is the line of least resistance that you can take. *Wimp,* get someone to do your power intro!)

When you are being power-introduced, I don't want you on the platform standing beside the person who is doing the introduction. You'll look like the little kid who can barely contain his excitement on Christmas morning. I want you seated to the side, and as the person delivers your power intro, I want you to be making eye contact, just like we talked about in chapter 2. Hold that eye contact long enough to form an opinion of each person you look at. I want you looking at that audience like a lioness on the prowl, sizing up the herd just before the hunt, deciding who and where you will target your interactions. I'm not saying you should get cocky, Just competently confident.

Let's move out of the arena of speaking to a larger group (more than three) and take this into a much more everyday situation, where you go in for a business meeting with one or a few customers in the room. The same rules apply. If one of the customers truly is your strategic business partner and you already have a relationship, ask that individual before the meeting if he or she would mind power-introducing you to the other members of the business team. If he or she is willing to, obviously, you have to get a concise power intro of yourself to that person well in advance of the meeting. Of course, after the power intro is finished, what you do is turn right around and thank your introducer for the strategic business relationship the two of you have established, and power-intro that person back to his or her own management team. As Abraham Lincoln said, "Everyone likes a compliment," and you will have made a business partner for life.

Here again, we have to deal with the "yeah, buts." Like, "Yeah, but Dan, these are new customers, and I can't get anybody to power-intro me." Well, it's the same as when you're speaking to the large group— you bring a business associate with you who can power-intro you to the customer. And then, as soon as that's done, you turn around and power-intro your business associate back to the customer. You'll be sure to point out why he or she is uniquely qualified to be an expert on this subject and how fortunate the customer is to have this person working on their account.

This is all pretty simple stuff. My observation in life is that most people do not do the pretty simple stuff themselves. So just remember, these power intros are so important they cannot be left to chance. They are highly scripted, and it is up to you to do the scripting. It is up to you to get the person who is going to power-intro you that script well in advance of the meeting. It is up to you to follow up to find out if he or she understands everything on the power intro or if there are questions to discuss. It is up to you to go for the highest Key Decision Maker you can get within that organization. It is up to you to go for the next highest if you can't get your first choice.

But hey! Is all this muss and fuss to get power-introduced really that important? Probably not. After all, it's only your career we're dealing with.

# Chapter 4

# The Script: Effective Content

*It takes about three weeks to prepare a good impromptu speech.—Mark Twain*

When talking about effective content, I ask people to envision the Golden Gate Bridge. Before you ever take the platform, you better make sure that you have a rock-solid foundation to build this presentation on. That foundation is your professional knowledge of your subject. If you do not know it and are not comfortable with it, and you do not have some conviction in your beliefs, it will be exposed when those adverse currents begin flowing in that business environment. And if you are not grounded in a solid foundation, you will be swept away.

But the bridge is also used to illustrate that you are with the audience on the near shore. What you are painting for them is the vision of the far shore, the promised land, where you and your organization can take the audience. The final phase is the implementation plan, the rolling out of your concept and how you will take the audience by the hand and walk them over these treacherous waters on this rock-solid foundation of a bridge to the far shore, which is their vision of where they want to go.

# The Seven Cs

So, what do Key Decision Makers, or any decision-maker who can make a difference, see as the basics of good content? The answer is found in the Seven Cs. And on them we must go a-sailing.

## 1. Concise

You already know what you have to say. The object is not for you to stand up and talk for the scheduled meeting time. The object is to get your value proposition out to Key Decision Makers as efficiently as possible and then proactively engage them to read their response.

## 2. Clear

What is the key take-away of your presentation? And by the way, how many key takeaways can your audience handle? If you said more than three, you are in danger of violating the first C. You better start slashing and burning the size of your briefing right now. Three is the absolute maximum that you can expect the audience to retain and walk out with and have a prayer they will act upon.

We've all seen what happens when an expert stands up and opens the fire hose, spewing out volumes, gallons of data. He hits the audience with all of it, and of course, none of it sticks, nor will it be retained. Decide up front what your key takeaway message is, and if you get the audience to walk out of the room knowing what it was, you have had success.

So how do you construct that content? The military has great terminology for it: tell them what you are going to tell them; tell them; and then tell them what you told them. What you told the audience is obviously your key takeaway for the meeting, and you have stated it to them three times—clearly and concisely. Indeed, it's just like dealing with your kids.

### 3. *Comprehensive*

How does your solution connect to the big picture? The bulk of my career has been in the health-care industry. Along the way, I have dealt with a lot pharmaceutical companies that are great at telling physicians, patients, and even insurance companies the fantastic features and benefits of their drugs. While that may apply to helping any individual get or feel better, they routinely fail to make it a comprehensive story. How will utilizing this particular drug improve population health overall and thereby reduce costs to the health-care system—which, left unchecked, will bankrupt our country as the Medicare population grows by ten thousand souls every day? That's the big picture: what is the patient's quality outcome if I use your drug, and how does it contribute to reducing overall expense?

And staying on that "comprehensive" theme, keep in mind Frederic Donner's (Chairman and CEO of General Motors, 1958 -1967) quote: "When you come right down to it, almost any problem becomes a financial problem." Gang, when you're talking business, you're talking financial problems, or at least financial objectives. You must *quantify* the value of your solution in terms that the customer uses to manage their business.

Those terms can be dollars made or saved; time, which can be translated into dollars; efficiency, which can be translated into dollars; productivity, which can be translated into dollars; expenses, which can be translated into dollars ... you get the picture, it's all about the dollars. Get your value proposition quantified for the customer, and you will always be able to concisely state your value proposition. Say, for example, "Implementing this proposal, which benefits both our organizations, saves your company $24M in the first year."

When you're quantifying the value of your solution to the customer, don't *you* be the one to minimize it. I hear people all the time saying, "I used conservative numbers because I didn't want it to get too big and not be believable." Well, if you want it to be believable, wouldn't you use the most likely numbers? I'm not saying make these up. You will in all probability be asked to defend how you established your quantification. But I'd sure rather say that my inputs to the value equation came from some recognized statistics on the web (and give me twenty-four hours, and I promise you I can come up with some basis to put together a quantification) rather than say, "Let me show you a really small impact on your business."

### 4. Controlled

You need to be in control. If you can't even take control of a simple business presentation, do you think I would ever trust you with my money? Time? Resources? Just take control. It will all go a lot smoother. (And actually, we know there is nothing simple about the presentation; you just have to make it appear that way.)

### 5. Consistent

Answers to questions better be the same. If you start changing the story in the face of related or repeated questions, open up that window and jump right out behind your credibility.

### 6. Committed

I'm reminded of a joke about a bacon-and-eggs breakfast: the chicken participated, but the pig was committed. Obviously we don't want your commitment going to this extreme, but this is another way of asking, are you accountable? If this plan doesn't come off as stated, do you just wash your hands and move on to the next project? Are you committed to your vision, your idea? Will you bear the consequences if this fails?

Make no mistake: if you are not personally bought in to making this happen, and every Key Decision Maker doesn't believe that you are, don't expect anyone else to give a rat's rear end either.

## 7. Creative

I know I don't even have to say this, but don't use the standard PowerPoint graphics. Be bold and radical. Go to the business store and buy a CD with pictures and incorporate those into your presentation. And not just pictures—come up with a theme. Over the years, I have used many different themes that resonated with clients:

- *Journey to Excellence* (based on Lewis & Clark's exploration of the Louisiana Purchase)
- *Into the New Frontier* (the US exploring space)
- *Soaring* (based on soaring in a sailplane)
- *Voyage to Success* (any sailing race you care to choose: for sales or account managers, I really like the *Vendee Globe*, the nonstop race around the globe ... solo!)
- *Smoke Jumpers* (Talk about somebody who is trained to be prepared to make on-scene decisions and successfully coordinate many disparate resources! These folks are committed.)

You can weave the lessons learned from any of these themes—such as strategic planning, preparedness, utilizing scarce resources, innovation, and effective communication under pressure—into crucial takeaways for the audience at the same time that you demonstrate your awareness of your need to manage them when the audience buys into supporting your vision. The list is endless, the impact tremendous.

# The Script

Now that we're done sailing the seven Cs, let's go back to your script. In building that great script, there are some principles you'll want to keep in mind.

*Quantify your proposal*

Let me ask you a little question: do you have more money than things your kids want to do? I have noticed that no matter how much flows around my house, there are always more demands than there are resources to meet those demands. It's the same in business or government. There is never enough money, and there are always other ways that it could be spent, other than with you.

So when you put together your presentation, you had better put together your quantification for exactly what investment is needed to go through with your concept and what the return to the bottom line for the customer will be. If you cannot state that in some form or fashion in numbers, you are asking those Key Decision Makers to reach a conclusion based on emotions or how much they like you. If you have managed to stick with this book thus far, you can tell by now that if I had to rely on that, I would be going on a diet real quick.

You have to be able to tie the outcome of the investment in you to the company's bottom line, impacting decision-makers financially. Whether it allows them to reach more customers with fewer dollars, to increase the margin on existing products, to sell more of existing products, to differentiate themselves from their competitors and charge a premium—you had better be able to state it in dollars (which can be derived from such things as saved time, increased efficiency, radical innovation that drives premium pricing, and higher reliability) and connect it to the bottom line.

### Focus on strategy

Tie your presentation to the big picture. Do not be dealing with some little tactical detail of the organization. How do I make my presentation strategic in nature? Well, I hop online, download the customer's annual report, and look at the news releases or listen to their quarterly analyst call to see what the senior management of that corporation is saying. Then I build my strategy right into their corporate strategy. I even brand the name of my proposal around their corporate strategy. Those Key Decision Makers might disagree with you, but they're going to be a lot less likely to disagree with their CEO and his or her vision for the future.

### Brevity is a blessing

The best data tells us that after about eight minutes, brain-slippage begins to occur. The audience simply gets distracted. For whatever reason, minds begin to wander. You have eight precious minutes to make your critical point and state your best case. After that, simply because of human dynamics, you are beginning to be a less impactful speaker—because the receivers are not working optimally anymore.

### Make good use of graphics

Envision a satellite picture of a hurricane. Now, attempt to explain to me the power of a hurricane verbally. You will not be many words into the process before you figure out that a picture demonstrates and explains the power and the impact of that hurricane ever so much more eloquently than you ever could. So plug the pictures into your PowerPoint presentation and use that to drive the impactful story.

But please, as I mentioned earlier, do not use the standard PowerPoint graphics. Go out and make the tremendous investment of a CD—or better yet, simply hop online and start cutting and pasting graphics that tell your story. Your listeners will definitely be more likely to pay attention to your message, and they will most certainly retain it better if you can show them a picture rather than say it with words.

*Wrap-up well.*

You already know what your wrap-up is going to be. You're going to tell them what you told them. Go right back to your power positioning intro statement about why you are there today and the results for the client's bottom line.

## Audience Response

You've given your presentation, and now you look at the audience, wanting to see if there is a reaction. Well, at least no one stood up and threw up. You are beginning to think they accepted it well. But still, there is silence in the room, and now you begin to hear the crickets chirp. At this point, you advance your PowerPoint one more, and your next slide says, "Next steps." How do you want to go forward from this meeting?

Once again, you begin to hear the crickets chirp. Perfect—merely step over to a flip chart (more on that subject to come in the next chapter) and write on it exactly the way you want the world to be. Who is going to do what by when? It may be that someone from the customer has to get you some data, and they will do that by a certain date, and then you will input that data into a contract that you will return to the customer by a certain date, and the customer will review and sign it by a certain date, so that the implementation plan may begin by a certain date.

Now, if nobody says anything from there and the crickets continue to chirp, you can just put up how you are going to go forward through the contract signing/project approval and implementation, since no one has objected.

But come on. As you know, along the way, someone will say, "Hey, wait a minute!" Most of us dread this moment. The push back! The objection! Oh *no*! It had all gone so well up until now. We dread this moment.

Listen very carefully to the objection, however. You are going to find out the real obstacles to your business agenda. It is critical to understand those before you can ever hope to move your agenda ahead or get key-stakeholder consensus and agreement to proceed.

After all too many meetings, we walk out and report back to the office, "Well, no one objected or stood up and threw up, so it must have gone well." Of course, as soon as we walked out of the door, that is when the Key Decision Makers turned to each other and said, "What a load of crap. That will never work around here. Clearly that clown doesn't understand our environment/culture/key issues/political reality/ organizational structure/previous investments ..." The list is endless.

That is the worst thing that could possibly happen to you. That is the last thing you want to happen. To walk out of that meeting without knowing what the objections are to moving forward with your recommendation is a disaster. So you will do everything you can to drive the customer to either agree to the plan or lay any objections out on the table. Do not fool yourself: if there is no commitment by the customer to do anything, your presentation or proposal just went nowhere.

In summary, avoid the common mistakes that people make in content:

- Do not do a data dump and force the customer to attempt to drink from the fire hose. There is no quicker way to lose your audience.
- Do not lose focus. Let customers know what it means to their business and repeat the two or three critical takeaways.

- Do not talk in generalities. Quantify your proposal. How can you expect customers to make a decision if they cannot see how it impacts their bottom line?

Always remember—great content takes time and thought. If you wait until the last minute to put it together, it will look like it was put together at the last minute. Let the content guide you, not control you. Be ready to go with where the customer's concerns are, and be darn sure to address those concerns.

# Chapter 5

# The Plot: Setting the Agenda

*Good leaders need a positive agenda, not just an*
*agenda of dealing with crisis. — Michael Porter*

The first thing we are going to do for our meetings, after we state the objective, is to reconfirm the time. The latest data tells us that 26 percent of meetings in corporate America start on time. That means that three out of four times we take the platform, we have less time than we initially anticipated.

So, if the meeting is typical for corporate America and late getting started, the first thing you'll say is, "Ladies and gentlemen, we originally had an hour scheduled for this meeting. Do we still have an hour?"

Probably, the Key Decision Maker will come back and say, "No, we only have forty-five minutes."

If you spent your whole meeting preparation time getting ready for a one-hour presentation, guess what, folks—you are royally screwed! And this is where that executive summary comes in handy, because you can cut to the chase and give the bottom line, explaining why you have come.

Have you ever been "in the zone" when you were up there doing a presentation? You just got out of the blocks, you are clicking along (literally, with your remote control), and the flow is going great. What happens then? Usually the door opens and the Key Decision Maker's assistant walks in and says that the decision-maker has a call from the CEO. Of course, you know who is going to get priority here.

So what do you do? Stand there and look dumb as the Key Decision Maker gets up and walks out? Start talking really fast in a vain attempt to cover your great presentation? Cancel the meeting? Come back another day? Forget all the time, effort, energy, and expense of getting all these people together?

Of course not! You already know from your executive summary what you are going to say to that Key Decision Maker as he or she has to walk out of the room: "In summary, what I want to leave you with today is how we can drive $24 million in savings to your bottom line over the next year." Always have that executive summary ready to go.

After about three decades in corporate American, I have figured out that basically there are three kinds of meetings:

1. *The Gapping Session:* This kind of meeting focuses on identifying the key issues that must be successfully overcome in order for the organization to succeed.
2. *The Solution Presentation:* This meeting asks, how are we going to overcome the key issues?
3. The *Wasted Meeting*: We didn't know what we were doing. We do not know if it was a gapping meeting to discover key issues, or if it was a solution meeting to address those key issues. All we know is we took up a bunch of time and have no clue what we are doing next. And I also know that I can't afford to be identified as having been the person directing that time-wasting event.

Let's consider those first two types of meetings. Master these, and you'll always be relevant to your customers, whether internal or external.

## The Gapping Session

This meeting might be conducted with your own internal management. Say you were considering an information-technology upgrade. The objective of that meeting would be to find out the key functions that a new IT system must be able to achieve. By extension, I think we can all figure out it would be pretty silly to try to design the IT upgrade before we determined the capabilities that the new system must support in the future.

If not an internal meeting, it is a meeting with customers, and the objective is to figure out what their key business issues are, because that is where we will want to focus our solution. We call these meetings "gapping sessions" because we are trying to understand where the organization is today, where it has to go in the future, and the difference between—the "gap."

Said another way—whenever you meet with Key Decision Makers, you want to ask them what is keeping them awake at night (about their business, not their kids or spouses). If I know what keeps that Key Decision Maker awake at night, I can begin focusing all my time, energy, and resources toward developing the solution. If I have a solution that overcomes the problem that keeps that Key Decision Maker awake at night, whatever it may be, chances are I am going to be a pretty valued business partner.

Once again, this goes for meetings with internal management or external customers. If it is a gapping session, you want to open the meeting by stating right up front that the objective today is to determine the key business issues that keep the organization from achieving its established business objectives. We are not there to fix the problem or figure out the solution. We are there merely to listen, clearly define, and gain buy-in from all Key Decision Makers that we do accurately understand the issue. People always say, "Oh, but Dan, I know the answer to the problem. I can tell them right now and save a ton of time, both for me and the customer." The problem with that is you lessen the value of your solution to the customer.

You should not attempt to fix the Key Decision Maker's problem at a gapping meeting. Multiple events can occur when you launch in with an immediate solution:

- The solution is based solely on your knowledge and recall ability at that moment in time.

- You may forget about the rest of the very important gapping process and immediately hone in on the issue that is of interest to you. It may not be a seriously important issue to the Key Decision Maker. You want to take time to ensure that you focus on the their most pressing problem. In that way, you will bring the highest valued solution and increase your influence with the customer.

- If the Key Decision Maker perceives that you merely threw out an off-the-shelf solution, they will value the input less. Leave the impression (and actually do it) that you have gone to a great deal of time, effort, energy, and thought in providing a solution to their problem.

- You may ultimately decide that you have better opportunities with more important accounts and therefore consciously decide not to invest your time and resources in this customer.

I was on my way home around the DC Beltway one winter night with a lot of snow and slush falling on the roadway, and sure enough, I found myself off in a ditch. In this age of wireless technology, I thought, *No big problem*. I pulled out my handy-dandy cell phone and was simply going to call for the tow truck to come pull me out and I would be on my way in no time. But when I turned the cell phone on, I found that my battery was dead. (Yes, I was an idiot. I did not have my car phone charger with me—it usually stays at home with my umbrella.) Now, batteries for my cell phone at the time cost approximately $44.95; however, at that moment in time and space, that battery would have been worth a lot more than $44.95 to me. Someone probably could have even valued that sucker somewhere above $1,000 for me at that moment.

It is the same with your solutions for your customers, whether internal customers within your company or external customers. If someone states a problem and you just reach in your pocket and pull out the solution, then and there on the spot, your listeners will think, *Hey, that was neat; as long as it is convenient, these people can help me out.*

No way would I give them the solution right then and there. I would listen to the problem. I would verify that I clearly understand the issue and that this was truly the key issue. Once I was sure I had it right, I'd confirm it again by saying, "To be clear, I understand this is the key issue?" And I'd get confirmation yet again from the customer.

Once I was positive I clearly understood the key issue, I'd say, "I'd like some time to get with my brain trust, connect with my network, find out how other people who have had similar problems have addressed this issue, and at minimum, even if I am not part of the solution, I will at least try to come back to you with some of the best practices that other people have implemented on how to fix these kinds of issues. Perhaps I can even arrange for you to speak to some of these folks who have successfully confronted similar issues." Then I'd wrap up that meeting by clearly stating, once again, what I understood the key issues to be and the next steps that I would take to put together a potential solution. Finally, I'd schedule a time when we all could reconvene to review that solution.

# The Solution Meeting

That, of course, leads us to the second kind of meeting: the solution meeting. At the solution meeting, guess what we present? That's right— our solution to the key business issue we have chosen to tackle. But we do not do that without first verifying again that the key issue is still valid.

One time I had gotten our organization on a schedule of the senior vice president for training of a huge Fortune 500 company. I'd had a previous gapping session with that person, verified with her that what we discussed was her key business issue, and gone off and put together, if I may say so myself, a darn good solution to that key issue. At the solution meeting, I stood up and confirmed the time that we had for the meeting and then reviewed the objective of the meeting—that it would be our solution to the key business issue she had previously discussed with me. I even followed the checklist down to the point of re-verifying the key issue, to which the customer stated, "Well, that may still be one of our problems."

That was good enough for me. I had spent all weekend putting together this presentation, and I immediately began to barrel into presenting my highly focused solution to what was originally stated as, and as far as I knew still was, one of their key issues. Thank goodness one of my partners went with me, because Ryan gave me the signal (we'll talk about signals in chapter 8) that something was going wrong and I needed to go to him for help.

Being mightily miffed that I was interrupted from giving my highly focused solution that I'd spent all weekend putting together, I looked at Ryan and said, "Ryan, did you have something to add?" to which Ryan made the brilliant observation of, "Well, Dan, I was just wondering, since this wasn't still Ms. Williams's number-one key issue, what *is* her key issue?"

As I gave my partner the stink-eye stare, Ms. Williams proceeded to tell us that over the weekend, the CEO of the company had made the decision to reorganize their sales force from geographically based to focused on vertical markets. But did I mention that I had a darn good presentation that I had spent all weekend working on?

There we were in the Key Decision Maker's office, and the solution presentation was no longer valid. What did we do? Well, we shut up, threw the presentation out, and went back to square one with a gapping session to find out what was now the key issue. Because, ladies and gentlemen, you already know I could brief all day on my focused solution, which fixed what was no longer the number-one problem, and she would not be nearly as interested in that as she would be in getting a solution to her new number-one problem.

So the message is, if you attempt to verify that the gaps are still valid and they have changed, forget your solution, shut up with the presentation, sit down, and start re-gapping the customer to understand what the key business issue keeping him or her awake at night is now.

If the Key Decision Makers you are dealing with are constantly having their key issues change between meetings, it does not take long before you figure out that these folks are squirrels, and guess what, they are not truly Key Decision Makers—or ones you can deal with, anyway. The best advice I can provide is to stay far, far away from those people. They are what I call time-sinks. They will endlessly chew up your time, never able to give definite form or shape to the problem, and the issues will continue to change. It is like trying to nail Jell-O to the wall. It is not going to happen, folks. Find the real Key Decision Makers in an organization to deal with. (And if this is an internal customer and the squirrel is your boss, good luck!)

# CHAPTER 6

# CHOREOGRAPHY: HANDLING THE LOGISTICS

*The officer who doesn't know his communications and supply as well as his tactics is totally useless. – General George S. Patton*

You are ready to state your objective, show your agenda, and confirm the time, and you are ready to go with your meeting, right? Of course not. Way before you even have anybody in the room, you need to decide on some logistics. As the military says about fighting battles, "Amateurs talk strategies and tactics. Professionals talk logistics."

Think back to the last time you were on a commercial airliner. As you were getting on, just before you turned right to sit down in your first-class seat, if you had looked to your left into the cockpit, you would have seen the pilots doing what? That's right—running a checklist. Now, I like to think they are not using that checklist because this is the first time they have ever flown that airplane. What I like to think is that they found that if they have a checklist and follow it religiously, they maximize the probability that this flight will go according to plan and without undue excitement.

You want to do the same thing for your meetings. The critical success factors for us to have a successful meeting fall into three categories: meeting preparation, managing the meeting distractions, and delivering the show from the platform.

Take a tip from pilots in that cockpit and use a checklist. We've all heard of Murphy's Law—everything that can go wrong, will go wrong. Well, Murphy was an optimist. It will be worse than that, folks! But if you create and use a checklist and add to it every time something goes wrong, at least your meetings will not be getting derailed for the same reasons.

Making a mistake is human. Making the same mistake over and over again is stupid and will be terminal to your career. Your checklist should include the following:

- *Room temperature*—if it's too warm, everyone will be falling asleep on you, particularly if it is an afternoon meeting.
- *Telephone*—not only are you going to remove the handset off the conference room telephone, you are going to disconnect it and hide it in a drawer so no one else can come in and put it back in its cradle. If you don't do that, I can promise you that right at the critical point of your presentation, that phone will start ringing, and it will probably be the clerk from out front looking for someone who is not even in the room. You do not need the distraction. Get rid of it.
- *Lights*—if a floodlight is shining on the projection screen or the fluorescent light is shining on it, it will wash out your presentation. Get there a little early and take the bulbs above the screen out so that it has a nice, dark background for your projection.
- *Flip charts with gridline paper*—I find that utilizing a flip chart (yes, those clunky out of date flip charts) creates the dynamic of working with your customers; whether internal or external meetings. Most people feel pretty good when they make a statement or suggestion and you record it on a flip chart in front of the audience. Validates them. Has their idea or suggestion called out and posted for

everyone to see. At minimum, they know you have heard and understand their position. Not a bad way to build an ally.

And when writing on the flip chart use big bold colors. As stated earlier, when doing your quantification for your audience be sure to do it in terms they use to measure and manage their business. So green for positive financial data. Red for negative. Once again, you in front of the audience, controlling the conversation; posting statements on the flip chart (and by the way, nothing has to go up on that flip chart that you violently disagree with, you hold the power of the marker and you can script it the way that best supports your solution). You are in control!

Another reason to get to the meeting room early is to grab that flip chart, dog ear a page so you can find it later in the meeting at a moment's notice, and lightly, in pencil; write out your entire quantification in one of the corners (depending on whether you are left or right handed). When the time comes in the meeting for you to show the audience how you derived your quantification, you step up to the flip chart, throw it open to your dog eared page and now in bold marker you begin doing the math. To your audience it will appear as a blank page. You of course are looking at your lightly written notes and transposing them into a bold quantification (to include all the math that begins to drive big numbers) right in front of your Key Decision Makers. When you turn back to the audience, their jaws are on the table, and your credibility is sky high.

Of course some critic will always ask: what happens if someone gets close to that flip chart and says "Hey! You had all of that written up there already." Well my response to that is, "You're darn right I did! I have an incredibly powerful quantification for you that I wanted to be sure I could get out concisely, clearly, and with maximum impact." And who do you want to do business with?

- *Your own markers* to go with the flip charts. (Do we even need to talk about the condition of the markers that are already in that conference / meeting room?)
- *Do Not Disturb sign* on the conference-room entrance door with your company logo on it. The entire message you want to send to everyone in that meeting is that there is nothing casual about this, and if this is the way you take control of a simple business meeting, can you imagine how well you will watch over whatever resources it is that you have been entrusted with to accomplish the company's business objectives?

As soon as you start the meeting, the first things that are on your checklist are:

- Confirm the time available.
- State the objective.
- Show your agenda.
- Ask: "Do we need to cover anything else today?"

For additional things to add to your checklist, just go to the bar with a bunch of your friends, sit down, and talk about the last business meeting you had. You will probably come up with at least another dozen items to include on your checklist. And shame on you if your meeting ever breaks down for one of those reasons.

## Room Layout

Now, let's consider the room layout for a presentation. If you don't do anything, what do you think you will get? That's right—the "usual and customary," which is the vertical room layout (see Figure 1).

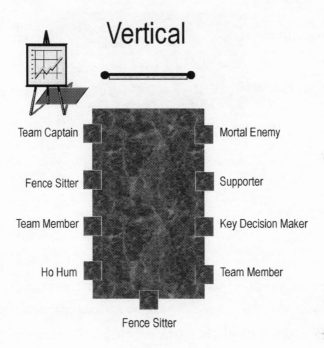

Figure 1

In this vertical layout, where does the Key Decision Maker in corporate America sit? You got it—at the head of the table. Who are you furthest away from in this setting? The Key Decision Maker. And who in the room is furthest away from your screen and platform, and where do you direct the presentation? That's right—the Key Decision Maker. So if you do not want to be the furthest removed from the Key Decision Maker, you better intervene to do something to change it. For starters, if at all possible, turn the room on its side and go for a horizontal seating (see Figure 2).

# Horizontal

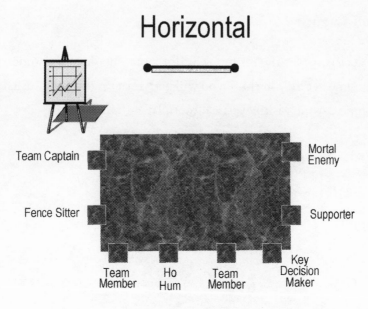

Figure 2

Look how much closer you are to wherever your Key Decision Maker sits than you were in the vertical layout. Look how big your platform is at the front of the room for you to move, engage, and address the audience. You are closer to all the participants, and you can have better interaction with all the participants.

This makes it much easier to handle any problem children. If somebody tells a neat little joke in a sidebar discussion and a lot of snickering and laughter breaks out, generally speaking, just moving over by it will cause it to stop. (If it does not, we will review the next steps you take in managing what we call those "ho-hums" in chapter 9.) With the vertical layout, you have to go stumbling down the side of the room, behind chairs and other seated people, to have a prayer of getting close enough to someone to shut down those sidebar discussions.

There's one other big reason to do the horizontal layout: it's different. Who would *you* want to do business with—somebody who does it the same old routine way everyone else has ever stood up and done a thousand times before, or someone who gets out of the box, takes some risks, engages the audience, and brings new thought to the way you are going to look at the world? I will leave you to decide that one.

Naturally, before we go any further, the "yeah, buts" come in. "Yeah, but Dan, we can't do that because the screen is at the front of the room." "Yeah, but Dan, that's the way the LCD projector is lined up." It's all a crock! There is nothing that says you can't turn the LCD projector sideways—or bring your own LCD projector, as I always do, because I do not trust anyone else's equipment. (That is on my checklist.)

Most rooms these days are either painted or papered a neutral color. As long as it is, with no bold prints, you can project right onto the wall. But even if there is a bold print, you have called and e-mailed ahead to the office assistant and asked to have a screen brought into the room. Hey, you're worth it. At a minimum, you can tape your flip-chart paper on the wall (that means you also need masking tape on your checklist) to make a screen.

Turn that room on its side, get closer to all the participants, expand your platform, and deliver your message with greater impact in a different environment. But whichever way your room layout goes, vertical or horizontal, you are not going to leave it to chance where people sit. And that brings us to the second way you will intervene to control the layout, and that is with name tents.

Let's jump right to the objections: "Yeah, but Dan, are you telling me that I am going to tell senior level people where to sit?" The answer is yes. In over twenty-five years of doing this, I have had two people decline to sit in the seat where I had a name tent placed. In the first case, the president came in, saw the name tents out, and said, "Well, I'm sorry, but that's my seat at the end of the table." He proceeded to pick up his name tent, move it to the end of the table, and sit down. (You know how shy these people are.) Having done that, he then proceeded to ask, "Why did you put out name tents, by the way?"

I responded, "We have a very high-value proposition for your team today, and I want to be sure we are set up to communicate with maximum impact and gain your feedback."

The president replied, "Well, it's neat to see that somebody actually thinks about details."

I'll take that hit. In the other case, the individual moved his name tent and said, "I'm going to sit on the other side because I'm deaf out of my left ear, and I want to be sure that my right ear is turned toward you." Once again, I received credit for showing attention to detail and driving my business agenda in a focused manner. So, get out of your box and try it ... it works!

Now, you are not randomly going to set those name tents down. Each one is going to have a purpose. Back on Figure 2, in the horizontal layout, you can see how I have it set up to create a direct line of communication between you and the Key Decision Maker, with your team member seated right next to that decision-maker, and his or her internal supporter on the other side in between the Key Decision Maker and any mortal enemy you might have on the customer team. Do not worry about the rest of those titles right now. We will cover those in detail in chapter 9.

Even if you get stuck with the vertical layout, you can see from Figure 1 that you are going to attempt to take control and get that Key Decision Maker to the optimal location.


## Microphones

A factor that can cause initial confusion in presentations is the use of microphones. As you figured out by now, I am going to do everything I can to avoid allowing anyone to chain me to a podium and restrict my movement on the platform. Whenever possible, I will request a wireless microphone so that I can be unchained from the podium. (By the way,

I will not even allow them to have the podium up there when they set the platform for me.)

If there are multiple speakers, you will wind up passing around wireless microphones as people exit from or take the platform. Of course, when speakers put on that microphone, the first thing they do is tap it and say, "Can everybody hear me?" Wow, what a powerful way to start your presentation.

To avoid this, as previously mentioned, I get there early, get the microphone that is going to be used, clip the microphone on my jacket, and do a volume check. I carry a marker pen, and I will put a little mark where my volume needs to be set whenever I do take the platform and have the microphone handed to me. When it is my turn, I walk up, take the wireless, and clip it on. I already know where to clip the microphone on my clothes, and then I adjust the volume to my mark. I am ready to start off with my high-impact statement, and I can skip the traditional, "Test, test—can everyone hear me?"

## Dressing

Before we move on, let's consider what the temperature is going to be in the room you are presenting in. Whatever that temperature is, it will feel fifteen to twenty degrees hotter when you take the platform, for the following reasons:

- There usually are more lights on the platform, which physically raises the temperature.
- You will have an LCD somewhere in proximity pumping out a lot of hot air that will increase that temperature.
- You will be nervous as heck, which tends to make you feel warmer, even to the point of perspiration.

The problem is, if you adjust the temperature to where you are comfortable on the platform, it will be cold enough to hang meat in that room, and the audience members will have purple fingernails. Make it comfortable for the audience, and you will be perspiring up on stage, where it is fifteen to twenty degrees warmer. To counter this, do not wear a heavy winter wool suit. You will look like Albert Brooks in the movie *Broadcast News*, when he finally has the opportunity to be the anchorman and breaks out in a monumental sweat. Dress light so that you will not perspire while operating under heat lamps.

As long as we are on the subject of dressing, avoid bold prints and plaids. Keep it business professional, and when in doubt, err on the conservative side. Ladies, in particular, pay attention to the accessories. I worked with a lady on one occasion who was a very powerful presenter, but she had bracelets on her wrist that were clanging together. It took the audience about thirty seconds to zero in on that and forget everything she was saying.

Accessories are not limited to jewelry. Avoid massive belt buckles, which will reflect lights that are shining on you. And if this is some sort of convention and you have one of those plastic laminated name tags either pinned on your lapel or hanging around your neck, take it off. The plastic will reflect the light and blind your audience.

I normally wear navy blue or black slacks, which buys me a little insurance—if I dump coffee or food on myself prior to taking the platform, there is less likelihood that it will show up against that fabric than if I had on my nice tan summer suit. You have enough things to worry about when you take the platform. You do not need to be concerned about whether people can see what you ate for lunch on your slacks or jacket.

## Seated Presentations

Something I am often asked about is the seated presentation. Does everyone remember Demi Moore and Michael Douglas in the movie *Disclosure*, where Demi tells Michael that the meeting starts at ten o'clock, but it really started at nine thirty, so naturally, Michael shows up late? As a result, he gets stuck with the broken chair. So here he is at a critical meeting with Key Decision Makers and everyone is sitting at a higher level than he is, and he also is sitting at an angle in this lousy broken chair.

How are you going to prevent that from happening to you? You are going to do the same thing for a seated presentation that you do for a standing presentation. You will get there early. The key takeaway from this book is if you show up at the scheduled meeting time, you lose. You are going to get to your meeting early and make sure you take control of that environment—not only to make sure you are in the seat you want but that all the other attendees are in the seats you want them in.

Just because you sit down for this portion of your presentation doesn't mean you can allow the energy level to drop, which will be your natural tendency. Interact with the participants just as if you were on the platform. Sit forward on your chair—you don't want to be leaning back like you're watching an NFL football game on a Sunday afternoon in Naugahyde Barcalounger.

You should also have your hands above the table. That is important for a couple of reasons. Number one, they are not underneath the table playing with things, which is quickly going to prove to be a distraction and get you in trouble. Number two, it shows the customer you are clear and aboveboard with where you are going.

In one of your hands, you want to have a quality writing instrument, because you are going to take notes. Now, when I say "quality writing instrument," I don't necessarily mean you need to have the Montblanc pen there, but you certainly do not want to be sitting there with your BIC nineteen-cent office special, either. As you have undoubtedly figured out by now, the question your listeners will ask is, who would *you* want to do business with anyway?

You are going to be taking notes because that shows the Key Decision Makers that you are listening, and it also sends out a subtle message that what they say is important enough for you to get it down on paper so that you can be sure to remember it. That is the real reason I take notes—because I have one of those old 286 processors embedded in my head, and if I rely on my poor memory for what was said at the meeting, when I get out of there I will have forgotten half of it. So I take notes to be sure I understand what the critical business issues are that we are going to go put a solution together for.

When you are seated, you may also have a tendency to brace your foot against the floor and start doing those nervous movements to get rid of all that excess energy. We have all been in meetings when that happens. You can even feel the floor or the table vibrate, as the person is there pressing his or her foot into the floor and doing little gyrations. So, no nervous movements. Remember, sit forward, hands above the table.

Finally, when you come to your high-impact statement, remember that you are not chained in that chair. Treat it just like a standing presentation. Get up and move to the flip chart and start scripting the end to the meeting just the way you want it. Do not let your energy go low just because you are sitting down.

## Contingency Planning

What happens if your key expert does not make it to the meeting? Do you say, "Oh, gosh, that is too bad, let's cancel the meeting and just do this another day." Obviously, in light of all of the peoples' time, effort, energy and expenses to get there, you are not going to do that. You want to be darn sure you do some contingency planning for the meeting in advance—in this case, to have a phone number you can call so the expert or a backup person can join the meeting via conference call.

What happens when the Key Decision Maker gets called away from the meeting? Time to quit again? The first thing you do is have your high-impact executive summary ready to go for that Key Decision Maker so he or she gets that critical takeaway while walking out the door. The next thing you can do after that individual is gone is determine whether you still have an audience that can make a decision. Make it a little bit of a challenge to their power in the organization. Can they make a decision without Mommy or Daddy in the room?

What are you going to do when the computer or LCD fails? Do you have your backup hard-copy handouts ready to go, and can you deliver the presentation effectively using only those handouts?

As you've figured out by now, there are easier things in the world to do than show up and take control of your meeting environment—but once again, what message do you want to send to the customer, and who would *you* want to do business with? Invest that time, energy, and effort. It will set you head and shoulders above your competitors.

# CHAPTER 7

# THE POWER (AND LACK THEREOF) OF POWERPOINT

*There's NO bullet list like Stalin's bullet list. – Edward Tufte*

Since the majority of presentations are done in PowerPoint today, let's review a few guidelines for its use. We already talked about being sure you get the lights above your screen turned out so that they do not wash out the colors in your PowerPoint slides. If it is a normal-sized conference room, you can easily pull a chair over and pop out the lights yourself. If it is a larger room, you will need to coordinate with the maintenance staff.

Undoubtedly, the first thing they will say is, "We cannot get those lights out," to which my response is, "So let me get this straight—if a lightbulb burns out, it is just out for eternity?" Obviously, they can get the lights out. It is extra work for them and they don't want to, but if you push them, they will get it done.

Sometimes I have to conclude the conversation by joking, "When I come in here tomorrow to do my presentation, I will have my BB gun with me. You can either take the lights out or I will take them out, but one way or the other, those lights will not be shining and washing out my PowerPoint screen."

Now, how many slides should you use in your presentation? Remember, the object of the meeting is not to listen to yourself talk, it is to get the other people in the room to talk. You already know what you have to say. The key is to get it out as concisely as possible and then read the audience for their reaction.

So, number one, you should plan to speak for no more than half of the total allotted presentation time. If you are scheduled for one hour, plan to speak for no more than thirty minutes from your PowerPoint slides. How many slides do you need for thirty minutes? The general rule is three minutes per slide. So if you have thirty minutes, no more than ten slides.

The presentation just got a whole lot tougher, didn't it? It's easy if I have all day to slide-whip you with a virtually limitless deck. It is very tough if I have only a few minutes.

We've all heard those stories about Mark Twain and how he said he would have written a shorter letter if he'd had more time. The same thing goes with your PowerPoint slides. Your tendency will be to put everything in the presentation so no one will have any doubt that you are the authority on the subject. (Unfortunately, after the eighth minute or the tenth slide, they've already fallen asleep.) If you consider your time constraints, there's no way you will be able to get through that lengthy presentation. The subtle message you will wind up sending to the audience is that although you command a lot of data and have a lot of information, you cannot control it or manage to communicate it in the allotted time.

Spend your time up front to convey what the key points, and only the key points, are that the audience needs to be made aware of. All else is superfluous details—which you have to know, but you don't have to bother the audience with. Managing all that is what they will be engaging you to do.

As to the words on your slides, they should be kept to a minimum. The words should only trigger for you what to say for each bullet. Do not put your entire briefing on the slide, or you'll wind up reading a novel to the audience, with a corresponding loss of platform power.

We talked in previous chapters about the power of graphics. Use them, and do not use the standard PowerPoint graphics. Go invest in another CD or a scanner to get good graphics that prompt you to deliver the high-impact words of your message. PowerPoint also has a lot of build capabilities in it, whether it be words that come flying in or noises that can be generated. The same rule applies to builds that applies to jokes: use them judiciously, and as soon as they become predictable, lose them.

Another caution on builds: if you put too many on there and you do not truly know your material, you'll wind up thinking your next advance of the remote device will take you to the next slide, you'll finish your summation of that slide, you'll hit your advance button, and out will come one more bullet. Generally speaking, only put builds on your most basic slides so that you know exactly when all the bullets have appeared.

You should also familiarize yourself enough with PowerPoint to be able to manage hidden slides. These allow you to put in data that you think customers or management may ask about, but if they do not ask about it, you do not want those slides appearing and chewing up your precious time on the platform, so you hide them. If management asks about critical details, you can pull that information up. If no one asks, you don't want to be the one to take them there.

How do you get your PowerPoint skills up? There are training companies in every major city. I liked one called Catapult (I do not get any kickback or have any business relationship with the company). If you need to take a PowerPoint course, call them. They will ask a few questions about your PowerPoint skills and slot you in one of five or six classes they offer. You'll go for one day from about nine a.m. to four p.m. When you walk out of there, your skills will be up to where you need them. They'll also provide you with a cheat-sheet book in which you can dog-ear all the critical things you need to know for future reference. This is a good investment of time to improve your skills, whether in PowerPoint, Excel, or anything else computer-related.

Finally, with PowerPoint, I should mention warping. If you are in PowerPoint's presentation mode, entering the number of a slide, such as "15," on the keypad and then hitting "Enter" will take you immediately to that slide. That can be a pretty powerful way to warp the audience around your presentation when a question comes up out of sequence of your briefing. Remember, you will have to go back, so you should be aware of which slide you are leaving so you can return to it immediately. Beside my PC, I have printed out on a piece of paper, in a big bold font, my slide numbers next to a brief description of each of the slides, so I can warp back and forth through my presentation without fear of not knowing where to go back to.

Talk with your colleagues about their techniques and tricks for PowerPoint. There are endless things you can do. You probably will never master all of them, but you should be aware of the few basics that will help you out during your presentations. Those few tricks will certainly enable you to project competence to your audience. Always remember, PowerPoint is not the show—you are the show. Use it to support you. Do not let PowerPoint dominate you.

# Chapter 8

# Supporting Cast: You Don't Have to Take the Platform by Yourself

*Teamwork is what makes common people capable of uncommon results. — Pat Summitt*

Whether you are giving a seated or a standing presentation, if you have business associates or allies in that room with you, utilize them to make sure your business agenda gets accomplished. The way you will do this is to have just a very few basic signals to allow your team to coordinate and drive your business agenda more effectively.

Don't make these signals too complicated, or you'll be like the batter trying to read the bunt signs from the third-base coach, standing there in the batter's box with the bases loaded, two down in the ninth inning. You have to keep the signals very basic so that you can recognize them when you are in the heat of the battle or the stress of the presentation.

One of the critical rules when someone is on the platform is, "No unrequested help." Most of us have seen what that looks like. Someone will be on the platform delivering a presentation and all of a sudden a boss or "friend" will pipe up and say, "Oh, excuse me, Dan, you got that wrong," and correct you!

*Thanks a lot, partner for cutting me off at the knees. Why don't we just drag my body out the door and put it in a dumpster out behind the office now, because my professional career just took a major hit!*

Now, instead of my ally interrupting me and causing me to lose all kinds of credibility, he or she merely needs to send me a signal—a signal that tells me that something has gone terribly wrong, I'm not aware of it, and I need to go to my team members for help.

The signal my team uses is standing a pen or pencil straight up and down. It is not noticed by the rest of the audience, but it can be easily seen by me (if I have made sure that my team members are positioned where I can easily see them) and lets me know that I have to go to one of them for help. I can now look at my team member and say, "Ryan, did you have a comment here?"

Ryan can then say, "Dan, I just wanted to be sure that last point came out clearly" and then make the corrected statement. He did come to my aid, but without detracting from my power or positioning on the platform.

A few other basic signals I've used with my team:

- *Putting my hand to my wrist* means time, and I've previously arranged with my teammates that I want to know when I'm halfway through the presentation, when I have five minutes left, and when I am going overtime. By the way, what happens if I go over? If I'm on a roll and the customer is with me, I sure do not want to be the one to break the continuity. But I do want to respect everyone's time and show that I am aware and in control. So I ask the audience. I explain that I'm happy to spend however long it takes to resolve our business agenda and move forward, but I want to be sure that I do not abuse their time—they are in control of whether they stay or not.

- *Hand to the ear* obviously means, "We cannot hear you in the back of the room." (If you are reading the eyes, you will be able to tell that. If people are leaning forward, they cannot hear you. If they are leaning back and give you the "deer in the headlights" look, the volume might be a little too loud.)
- *Finger into the palm*: You're onto something, dig deeper.
- *Finger roll*: They've got it—move on.
- *Eye contact*: If you're asked a question by a Key Decision Maker, make eye contact with the appropriate person on your team who would be the expert to answer that, and if he or she gives you that very slight nod, you know to go to that person. If you don't get the nod, you will either make the decision as to whether you are going to answer the question or say, "We will investigate that and get back with you." There's nothing wrong with saying that, as long as it is like everything else—not becoming predictable. If you use that statement too many times, you really did not know your material or have a good understanding of your audience when you took the platform.

These are just a few basic signals. You can figure out which ones you need for your team to operate effectively. I encourage you to keep them very few and very simple—otherwise, in the heat of the battle, you will begin to have a communication meltdown.

Now, obviously, everything you have done up to this point is to try to project competence and instill confidence in your audience that they want to do business with you. But one of the key places that it all breaks down and falls apart is at the end of the meeting when the presenter typically says, "Are there any questions? Thanks for coming today." Well, that sure is a great way to wrap up, isn't it? What you want to do instead is ask, "What are the next steps? Where do we go from here?"

When you start hearing those crickets chirp, you are going to step over to the flip chart, throw it back to your previously dog-eared page, which has "Next Steps" written up there, and start painting the world exactly the way you want it to be. Someone will either stop you and say, "Wait a minute, Dan, we are not ready to go to that step yet," or you will script out the action items for the follow up e-mail.

More likely than not, it will be the former. And you have just uncovered the issue that is going to keep your agenda from moving forward, and that is precisely what you want to talk about. If it is the latter, you just listed the content for the after-action e-mail that will state who is going to do what by when.

If someone is going to object to an action item, I want that person to have to state it in that meeting, in front of peers and management. I do not want it to come up later when the e-mail goes out and the person exclaims, "Well, I never agreed to that." Once you have those next steps firmly documented, to include who is going to do what by when, you are on the way to implementing your business plan for success.

As our world becomes more and more of a global economy, we get more and more of a class of people who I have a tremendous amount of admiration for—the immigrants to our country. We get the best and the brightest. We get the people who have the initiative to get up off their duff and come to this country and learn their profession in a foreign language. I am in awe of these people.

One of their chief barriers can be their native tongue and the heavy accent when they speak English.

If English is not your native tongue, or you work with someone who has a heavy accent, you want to be sure that you slow down and emphasize the vowels in the words while you are presenting. By doing this, you will ensure that your audience can understand your message.

Whew! This is a lot of work for one meeting. But hey, remember, this shouldn't be any big deal—it's only your career.

You are just about ready to run your successful meeting, but there is one other chapter we should cover before we go on. Well, not everyone has to cover it. Many people work in a totally collegial environment where they will not have to worry about this next chapter. If you are one of those, do not bother to read it. However, if you'll be presenting in an environment in which people tend to be cantankerous or take exception to what you say, you might want to learn more about handling a tough crowd.

# CHAPTER 9

# THE TOUGH CROWD

*It has been my philosophy of life that difficulties*
*vanish when faced boldly.—Isaac Asimov*

I magine the slaves walking into the Roman coliseum—lambs to the slaughter. The very thought of it conjures up career-ending nightmarish tales of when some colleague went before a tough crowd and his or her career went down in flames. It was all over, all downhill from there.

Now, we all know most people's managers are not like that. Most of them are real polite, real considerate, and are always willing to show exceptional patience when dealing with subordinates in a business presentation format. But if you happen to be one of those rare exceptions who has Type A personalities around your organization, with CEOs and senior VPs who can be just a little pushy and demanding in meetings, perhaps you want to skim this chapter. After all, if you want to be taken seriously, if you want to project competence and instill confidence, you better be able to take control of the situation and handle the tough crowd. You must be able to *carpei audientiam*—seize your audience!

My experience of the world has been that the tough crowd splinters into four groups.

- supporters
- ho-hums
- fence-sitters
- mortal enemies

If you are fortunate (or you take the time to orchestrate it), you will have some supporters. There will definitely be some ho-hums at the meeting. The core of most organizations is the fence-sitters. And finally, there will be a mortal enemy out there—that person just waiting to "make your day." If you want to be taken seriously, you better be able to handle each of these types, or the tough crowd will take you down.

## Supporters

It's great to have supporters, and you very definitely need them—the more the merrier. However, in your interaction with Key Decision Makers, the danger you face with supporters is that you will be drawn to them like a moth to the flame. It is comfortable next to your supporters. They are smiling, they are nodding; it feels real good standing close to them, and when you ask them a question, they give a positive, supportive response.

But do not let your supporters lull you, and do not let your whole presentation get focused only on addressing your supporters. It will be obvious to the rest of the management team that you are nervous about leaving your comfort zone. They'll assume you can't handle the heat of facing tough executives and getting your concise value proposition out.

It will be interpreted as a sign of weakness and a lack of conviction or confidence.

If these Key Decision Makers believe that you only have one or two people from their team who are in agreement with you, they're going to have doubts. Big doubts. In the worst case, if you are continually going to your few supporters, you'll ultimately wind up compromising those supporters' credibility with their own team.

That is in no way to say forget about your supporters. You will come to them at appropriate, critical times, so you definitely need to keep them with you.

## Ho-Hums

The ho-hums are the easiest group to deal with. We all know who the ho-hums are in our organization. They are the ones who show up for the jelly doughnuts at the meeting. They are reading newspapers, texting, i-surfing, perusing e-mails, doing anything but paying attention to you. After all the time effort and energy you put into this presentation, that can piss you off!

But ask yourself these questions: Are ho-hums true Key Decision Makers in their organizations? Would they ever make a decision? And if they did, would anyone listen to them? Nope, nope, and nope.

These are the straphangers. They only showed up so they could get doughnuts and escape their cubicles; after all, they might have to do work if they stayed at their desks. You offer an escape and doughnuts! Maybe even lunch if they time it right.

They are going whichever way the flow goes and offering the least resistance. If whatever those ho-hums are doing is not taking away from your platform power and your business agenda, leave them alone. They are not worth your time.

The rule with ho-hums is to forget them—unless they are distracting your audience. The moment they engage in behavior that is disruptive, you have no choice but to intervene or be viewed as a tremendous weakling. How do you intervene with the ho-hums or anyone else who is acting as a distraction?

I will give you the worst scenario I've encountered during my career. I was doing a presentation before my executive vice president (at the all-important, career make-or-break internal meeting) when someone in the meeting, who I actually thought was my friend, pulled out his clippers and began to clip his fingernails. I felt as if he might as well have just walked up and spit on me. Could I allow this behavior to go on without detracting from my agenda? Just hope no one notices? He's *cutting his fingernails*, for God's sake. Everyone was noticing!

My listeners were not going to get the full impact of my value proposition. They were not going to remember what a great business case I delivered, how well thought-out it was, how it was going to drive results to the bottom line. The only thing they were going to remember was my pathetic attempt to push on in the face of this like nothing was happening. I was about to become a company legend ... or more precisely, a company joke.

I made the determination that if I attempted to ignore this, the entire management team would conclude that dealing with Dan was tantamount to dealing with a milquetoast—and who would you *not* want to write investment checks for anyway?

I have already talked about the power of the platform and how your movement or pointing at someone can put him or her on the spot. You don't want to overreact and turn your intervention into an attack, which would cause your audience to rally to the ho-hum's defense. (After all, it could be them you attack next. You might turn on them!) Given that restriction, what are you going to do?

Here is my foolproof technique. Remember earlier in the book when I said, "When in doubt, what do you do? You go to the audience." In this case, you go to the audience by asking the ho-hum a question. Just ask the person who is engaging in disruptive behavior what he or she thinks about the topic that you are talking about right now. We all know what is going to happen. That person's head is going to snap up, eyes big with that "deer in the headlights" look, and a surge of adrenaline will go through his or her system.

So when my "friend" began clipping his fingernails, I moved toward him (remember, move toward your problems in life not away from them). When merely moving in his direction did not get his attention, I asked him a question. His head snapped up. Naturally, he was not paying attention, and his response was something like, "Well, whatever the rest of the team thinks." While responding, he had stopped clipping his fingernails, so I returned to my presentation. And do you know what he did then? He returned to clipping his fingernails.

*What do I do now?* I thought frantically. He didn't respond to the movement. He didn't figure out that my question was an intervention in his behavior. He didn't get that I was trying to save both of our careers (well, let's be honest, he was a ho-hum—he didn't have a career to save). *What do I do now?*

What I wound up doing was exactly what I did before—I asked him another question. Again, his head snapped up, and again he gave his typical noncommittal answer. But a switch did go on in his head, a flicker of recognition—I could see it because I was certainly reading his eyes. With that second question (actually, just the same question asked twice), I had instantly negotiated with him. If he engaged in clipping his fingernails, I was going to ask him a question.

It was not an attack, it was not overly aggressive. It did not alienate the audience, but it did shine a spotlight on the individual to let him know that I knew exactly what was going on—that he was not paying attention to my presentation and I was going to call him on it.

Now the rest of the audience obviously knew what was going on. You could even hear a couple of snickers going around, but the very clear and powerful message that I sent was that "if you are not here to discuss our agreed-upon business agenda, stop wasting my time. I, on the other hand, do have to get on with delivering my agenda and delivering my value proposition, and I will not tolerate anyone showing discourtesy or a lack of professionalism in operations I am involved in." Done ... or as I really like to say, "D-U-N. Dun!" Ho-hum contained.

## Fence-Sitters

The third type of person you will have to deal with is the fence-sitter. These are individuals who do carry weight within the business organization. As a matter of fact, in most organizations, which are consensus-driven, these people are the vital, solid citizens who have the corporate knowledge base of past experiences, best practices, and pitfalls to avoid. They are truly attempting to make the best decision for the organization.

In all but the most hierarchical or dictatorial organizations in corporate America, the senior Key Decision Maker will turn to trusted lieutenants before making a decision. Most of us have been in the room and witnessed this event at one time or another. The decision-maker actually goes around the room asking these trusted advisors, the lieutenants, the fence-sitters, "What do you think?" Rarely do I have a Key Decision Maker who goes against a strong consensus recommendation from this group. If you get the fence-sitters on your side, you'll get over 90 percent of the decision you want, and I'll take that batting average.

This is your chance to work. This is where you will win over that consensus center of gravity that will help you overcome those mortal enemies out there and gain buy-in to your value proposition, whether from internal management or external customers. You want to interact very heavily with the fence-sitters. You want to be sure to ask them a lot of questions. Are they with you? Do they have objections? Do they agree?

Whenever a fence-sitter comes out with a positive statement, you for sure want to reinforce it and, of course, at that time, go to your supporter as well to get that person's endorsement that you are on the right track. Use your platform power to build these people up and reinforce when they are going in the direction you want them to go in. Above all, interact with their eyes and address their concerns. If you pull the fence-sitters to your side, you will get endorsement of your value proposition. You will get approval of your business agenda.

## Mortal Enemies

And now for those mortal enemies. The first thing is, do not overreact. Not everyone who asks you a question or challenges you on something is a mortal enemy. He or she could be a fence-sitter who is just attempting to understand more clearly so as to know which way to lean in the decision that is to be made.

Mortal enemies are those people who are really out to torpedo you and your idea. Usually, mortal enemies are right there in your face and pretty open and boisterous about it. But the most deadly kind of mortal enemy is the one who lays in the weeds and never lets you know it. So you have to make a conscious effort to be sure when you are working the audience that you go to all of the Key Decision Makers with that good eye contact and read them. Are they with you? Are they endorsing this? Do they have concerns?

You need to actively seek out, engage, and find out where everyone is on the agenda, because the worse thing is to let mortal enemies sit there without declaring themselves, and after you leave the room, they begin to do their damage. You know the statements that will be used—"That will never work here," "We have heard this all before," "I do not have any faith in these people." If those are the objections, you need to get them brought out while the meeting is in session so that you and your team can address the facts rather than being ghosted with hearsay after you have left and are not around to defend your position.

This is the reason we conclude our meetings by going to the flip chart and scripting the world the way we want it to be. Who will do what by when? This makes it almost impossible for mortal enemies to play that snake-in-the-grass strategy and emerge only after you leave. They must emerge now or witness the after-action e-mail being constructed before their eyes. Though you probably dread the emergence of the mortal enemy, it is a good and essential thing. You will know the obstacle to implementing your value proposition.

If it is the more common kind of mortal enemy who is very in-your-face about it, what do you do? Well, first of all, you are usually terrified, and that can often lead you to overreact and get in a verbal exchange that turns into a he said/she said thing. Key takeaway: do not allow the mortal enemy to engage and draw you into a protracted debate on the pros and cons of your agenda. Yes, you have to address it, but ask yourself, will you ever win the mortal enemy over? The answer is obvious—you will not. So do not expend all your time, energy, and effort in trying to do that.

If the mortal enemy is *the* Key Decision Maker for the customer, you may have to come to the conclusion that this just is not a business battle you can win (but not before you attempt to win over the fence-sitters; remember, it is very unusual for the Key Decision Maker to go against the advice of trusted lieutenants), and therefore you never wanted to engage in this battle to begin with. Shame on you for not having identified that at an earlier stage.

In dealing with classic mortal enemies in a live meeting, let's first consider a couple of questions. What are their personalities typically like? These are people who are just gloomy. As a matter of fact, they go around with a little thunderstorm cloud over their head, perpetually in a bad mood, perpetually short-tempered, perpetually raining on everyone's parade, perpetually brusque with everyone they deal with.

This leads us to the second question. How are mortal enemies typically viewed from within their own organizations? Very much the same as they are perceived from outside the organization—as cantankerous, complaining, foreboding, negative personalities. And guess what, folks? Their internal colleagues are even more sick of dealing with them than you are.

Another key takeaway is that if you are viewed as attacking the mortal enemy in the meeting, even if that individual is provoking you, colleagues will close rank around him or her. The reason they will do this is because they could be next. You might turn on them. As long as you do not turn and attack mortal enemies, though, you will be able to use their colleagues' frustration with that mortal enemy to your benefit.

First, you have to smoke mortal enemies out, and second, you have to avoid overreacting to them. Overreacting is just what they want. It gives them the opportunity to dominate the conversation and, hence, your agenda. By "overreact," I mean that you allow mortal enemies to dominate your time, conversation, and audience interaction.

You get sucked into a ping-pong match. You send a good point over the table, and your enemy hits it right back at you. You send another good point over the table, and your enemy hits it right back again. How long are you going to do this before you realize that no matter what you send over the table, it is coming back with a big objection attached to it? You will never win this ping-pong match. Stop trying! That is not your objective.

Once you know who your mortal enemies are, try not to engage them extensively; instead, try to minimize them. Here is how you do it. When the mortal enemy challenges you, the first thing you do is go palms-up. Remember, you do not want to be in attack mode. You want to be in working-with mode and move slowly toward the attack, using the LAER model.

# The LAER Model

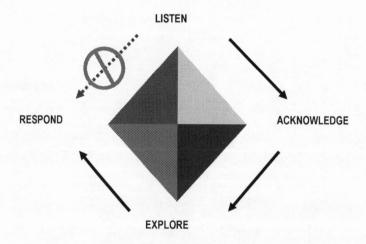

Figure 3: The LAER Model

The LAER model is a great process that I wish I had learned a lot earlier in my life. It works in both a professional and a personal environment. If you get nothing else from this book, remember that when you get challenged, run the LAER model. The model has four steps.

## Step 1: Listen

Go palms-up and listen—just listen. Actively listen, because no matter who it is, even if it is a mortal enemy, on occasion he or she may have a valid point.

But even if your enemy's points are not valid, what do people want most of all? They want to be heard and will never cease broadcasting until they feel they have been heard and understood. Go back to our first key takeaway in the book: When in doubt, what are you going to do? You are going to go to the audience.

In this case, you are going to go to the challenger, palms-up, and ask him or her, "Let me be sure I clearly understand. Why do you say that?" Then actively listen to the response. You may pick up legitimate reasons for concern.

If you are a classic Type A personality like I am, you'll practically have to gnaw your tongue off while you try to listen. You'll be dying for your chance to respond. If the mortal enemy comes out with an objection, you'll come back with two reasons to override that objection. If the mortal enemy has two objections, you'll have four reasons to override those objections. And so the ping-pong match begins. Back and forth. Back and forth.

The bottom line is, it does not matter what you could go back at that enemy with—you are not ready to respond. This is the lesson I wish I had learned earlier in life. All you have to do is shut up and listen, and then move on to the second step of the LAER model.

## Step 2: Acknowledge

Notice *A* does not stand for *agree*. You merely acknowledge. People want to be validated. They want to know that their pain is heard and felt by others. So after I have been attacked and said to the mortal enemy, "Why do you say that?" I let that person go off. I let my enemy vent, but I actively listen.

After he or she has finished, I then acknowledge what was said. "I can understand how you might feel that way. Time and resources are compressed. Here you are with me while other work is piling up."

Next, after you have acknowledged the enemy's point of view, you get to respond, right? Wrong!

## Step 3: Explore

For the moment, you merely want to explore. This is where, if you have a mortal enemy who you have determined really does have some valid reasons, you may want to start exploring potential solutions with that individual. On the other hand, if you did not think the reasons are all that valid, you want to open up that exploration to the entire audience—but not with a random question to the entire group.

You want to explore the issue first with your supporters. Go palms-up to your supporters (you'll know who they are if you've been reading the eyes) and ask, "How do you view this issue?" My overwhelming experience is that 90 percent of the time, if you've been professional with your listeners, they will rally to your defense. I kid you not—90 percent of the time.

Why? Two powerful factors. First, remember earlier we talked about how the audience really does want you to succeed. They know firsthand the stress and angst you are under. They feel for you. They actually are in awe of the way you are calmly handling this attack.

And secondly, they despise the mortal enemy even more than you do. They would actually love to give the mortal enemy some comeuppance. They just can't be seen as being disloyal to the organization when they do it.

That's where merely turning to your supporters and giving them the opportunity to broadcast will get the audience stating for themselves the value your proposal or recommendation can bring to their organization. It works! If you do this professionally, your supporters will say something like, "Well, despite [the mortal enemy]'s concerns, I do believe this brings value to us."

Now, as soon as you get any statement like that, you will be overwhelmingly tempted to go back to the mortal enemy and say, *"Aha! What do you think now?"*

And your enemy is going to say, "I still think it's a crock!"

*Do not* go back to the mortal enemy. You will never win that person over. Instead, if you have another supporter in the meeting, you go immediately to that colleague and get a strong supporting statement. If you are so fortunate as to have additional supporters, you now go to each of them in turn to get their strong supporting statements.

> Be aware that if you have supporters, or even fence-sitters, who you do not openly check in with and give an opportunity to speak, they will begin to resent you. They will feel ignored in a meeting that broke down into that ping-pong match between you and the mortal enemy, and all the time they wanted to support you. *Now* is when you *must* go to your supporters.

Once you've gotten strong supporting statements out, it's time to check in with those critical fence-sitters. You'll never have a higher probability of getting the decision to go your way than right after strong audience support. You now go to those trusted lieutenants and provide them with an opportunity to weigh in on the value your proposal has to their organization.

And if the mortal enemy's points are just a bunch of BS, chances are some of your supporters, and very possibly the fence-sitters (who the mortal enemy has now lost credibility with because he or she is arguing from emotion, not from solid facts), will come on line and say something like, "You know, frankly, that really isn't all that big of an issue to us. I can see how we could benefit from implementing this within our organization."

Whatever the reaction, guide the audience in exploring the value your proposal has for them. You may well take notes or write some suggestions up on the flip chart. Validating what people say in this way is going to gain their buy-in to your solution. The whole time you are exploring with the audience, you might actually get good ideas, solutions, and recommendations, and what better solution to implement than one the audience wants? At minimum, you've bought yourself time to think about what your response is going to be, and you're collecting pertinent information concerning the issue from the audience that you can build into that response.

### Step 4: Respond

After you have listened, after you have acknowledged, and after you have explored potential solutions, then and only then do you want to think about coming back with your response. "So what I'm hearing is that while there can always be conflicting priorities, it does sound like this solution would benefit the team. So here's what we'll do." And start scripting the world exactly the way you want it on the flip chart.

It almost makes me cry when I think of all the pain and agony this model could have helped me avert in my life if I had used it at an earlier stage. You never know what you don't know, and there is nothing I can do about not using it when I did not know about it, but shame on me if I don't use it in the future going forward. And shame on you if you don't use it also. By running the LAER model, you will, in all probability, help diffuse the situation, clarify the issue, and come up with a solution.

At an absolute minimum, even if the decision does not go your way today, you will walk away with your credibility intact and the audience in awe of how your handled that toughest of business situations. And who would *you* want to do business with in the future?

Another great technique that the LAER model builds upon for you is letting peer pressure work. Remember that chances are, if this is the mortal enemy who has a little black cloud hanging over his or her head, that individual's peers are more sick of dealing with that behavior than you ever will be. Oftentimes, the peers will let it go for a while and finally say to the mortal enemy, "You know, maybe we should just move on with this. We are never going to resolve it to your satisfaction, so we're just going to have to move on anyway."

When this happens, oftentimes mortal enemies gets frustrated, and on more occasions than not, they find reasons to excuse themselves from the rest of the meeting, usually concluding with, "Do what you want."

One time when this occurred, one of my teammates tried to stop this enemy from leaving. So great was the desire to win the mortal enemy over that my team member didn't want that person to leave! Do not stop your enemies, because when they leave, you win. You got rid of your mortal enemy, and if you still have your Key Decision Maker in the room, you are ready to move forward with getting buy-in for your solution.

If you still have not taken care of the problem, you can try one more thing: dumping a little gasoline on the fire.

One time I was in a negotiation where the mortal enemy *was* the Key Decision Maker for the customer. The mortal enemy was the program director. In the meeting, he actually called us crooks and thieves. All I could see was the world falling apart. Here we were with the customer, accused of being crooks and thieves. How were we ever going to close this deal and move forward to implement our solution?

Fortunately, there was a wise old gentleman on our team who leaned forward and said, "We would like to ask you to do one of two things: refer criminal charges to the appropriate authorities or retract your statement, because we are not crooks and thieves."

Well, the mortal enemy said, "There will be no apologies from us. As a matter of fact, this meeting is over." Then he got up and took the rest of his team with him, and they left the room. The only thing that was racing through my mind was, how in the world was I going to go back to my boss and explain to him how things had gone so terribly wrong?

After they left, this wise old gentleman on our team turned and said, "We've got them." And when you think about it, we did. The mortal enemy had acted unprofessionally. All we had to do was request a meeting with his management. If that meeting had taken place, we were going to walk into his management and say, "We are a little confused. This individual who you designated as the person we work with on this project has called us crooks and thieves, but refuses to produce any evidence to substantiate that claim, and also refuses to retract the statement."

That mortal enemy was in a position where he could not afford to be in trouble with his senior leadership. He had acted unprofessionally, and when the chips were really on the table, he did not want that information going to his boss. I will not bother you with all the other boring details. Suffice it to say, from that incredibly disastrous start, we wound up signing the largest single-year contract in the history of the company up to that time.

So if you have one of those valid mortal enemies, go ahead and dump enough gasoline on that fire to let your enemy have that explosion, and chances are, you now have a big one to hold over his or her head.

If that still doesn't work, what do you do? Before you watch the whole thing go down in flames, before the whole process collapses, you want to keep your cool, and you do not want to panic. It's like the old sports analogy: you are doing the two-minute drill, and you have to move down the football field and score to win the game. The quarterback takes the snap; the linebacker comes clean and buries the quarterback for a fifteen-yard loss.

What do you do now? Do you frantically try to recover the situation then and there? No, ladies and gentlemen, you call a time-out! You stop this train wreck right now by saying, "It looks like we have some significant issues to overcome. What I would propose is, let us take your concerns, conference for a few minutes, and then we'll come back to you and let you know what we might be able to do to address those issues."

You can also ask the customer to do the same thing. But, even beyond the time-out, if you decide this is it, if you decide this is make-or-break, if you decide it is now or never, then and only then you may want to consider going for the throat of the mortal enemy. If you have the data and the business facts to back you up and bombard them, you may decide to go shred them. But I caution you: this is thermonuclear warfare, and I would do it only in the event that it is all or nothing on this day, at this hour, and the discussion cannot be postponed or rescheduled.

Ultimately, if the audience doesn't see the value, if it is just not your day, if it just is not going to happen, if you just are never going to move forward, you may be at the stage of saying, "You know, folks, it looks like it just isn't going to work out. I would like to have been able to implement a solution that drove [your quantification] to the bottom line, but I can see I've not done a good job of positioning my value proposition with you. So thanks for your time. We will have to get on with life somewhere else. I realize you will too. Maybe we can work together in the future." You bag it, and walk out on the high ground.

There are other places to make your livelihood.

*Speak when you are angry, and you will make*
*one of the best speeches that you will ever regret.—Anonymous*

# CHAPTER 10

# WHAT CALL PLAN ARE YOU ON?: PHONES AND E-MAIL

*Ninety percent of all problems are the result of*
*poor communication. – Dan H. Brooks*

T he final things you need to think about when it comes to
projecting competence and instilling confidence are written and
telecommunication messages. Let's start with that great bugaboo today,
the telephone—specifically, the cell phone.

You can scarcely go to a restaurant these days, no matter how nice
it is, without having your meal interrupted by somebody's cell phone
ringing. Now, ladies and gentlemen, if we are busy eating lunch or
more specifically, if we are busy eating lunch with someone else, and
especially if we are conducting a business meeting with someone else,
why do we feel compelled to answer that cell phone in the middle of
lunch? Think of the very powerful message you just sent to the person
you were having lunch with, whether it is a friend or business associate:
"I am sitting here face-to-face having a discussion with you, but this
phone is more important."

I guarantee you that the CEOs and the major power players these
days do not sit down to their meals and feel compelled to allow a cell
phone to interrupt them. It is the same thing in meetings with *your*

business associates. What does it make people feel like when you are in the middle of a discussion, the phone rings, and you decide to answer it?

I know I'm completely out of touch with the millennials on this topic. My daughter, a very successful millennial, tells me that answering the phone or texting during an ongoing interaction is no dis in this day and age. I'm the dinosaur. Make your own call on this one (pun intended).

I once had a product vice president of a company, Hector, come to me and say, "Dan, we have some folks who really need some communications help, specifically our vice president of sales." He asked me if I could help this VP, whose name was Wayne. Naturally, I said I would be happy to try.

I suspected that Wayne had some problems prioritizing when he missed three scheduled telecons with me. On that third scheduled call, he actually answered the telephone and then proceeded to tell me he was too busy to talk. I thought, *Why the hell did you answer the phone?*

Finally I said, "Wayne, I am willing to work with you, but I am not willing to do it via cell phones because that is breaking down. So what I will do is, I will meet with you face to face." He agreed to that, and at the appointed hour, I went to his office.

I had not been seated in his office for more than two minutes before his phone rang, and he proceeded to immediately answer it. *Of course*, I said to myself, *clearly, this is a very important meeting to Wayne, and I am a very critical person to him.* But to my further amazement, when Wayne answered the telephone, he told the other person that he did not have time to talk right then and would have to call back.

When I came out of the meeting, I went to my friend Hector and said, "You know, it is no surprise to me that Wayne cannot manage a sales force. This guy cannot even manage his own calendar."

The message is, if you are not ready to talk on the phone, whether you are placing a call or receiving it, do not talk on the phone. If you are in conversation with someone else, you are not ready to talk on the telephone. This is like dealing with your kids: you are either training them, or they are training you.

I want to establish the concept that I cannot be reached at the whim of anyone who touches my name on his or her iPhone's contacts list. That is being too accessible. The power players in corporate America are not too accessible, particularly to underlings. Be sure you prioritize your activities and do not allow that cell phone to become an auto-interruption device (unless you need it to escape from a useless meeting—but that is a technique discussion for another day).

Once you have decided you are going to place a call, be sure to run three things through your mind before you touch the screen:

1.  What am I going to say if the person I am calling answers live?
2.  What am I going to say if I get the person's voicemail?
3.  What am I going to say if I get the person's executive assistant?

There is no greater way to lose credibility or presence than to leave long rambling voicemails that go nowhere and ultimately even have you backing up and repeating some of the same information—meaningless information—more than once.

Pre-think what the key point is that you wanted to get across and leave that—and only that—on the voicemail with recommended times for that person to contact you or when you will attempt to contact him or her again. You will not be able to leave a life-altering, impassioned plea on voicemail, so don't try. If the person (or his or her assistant) answers live, then obviously you know to have your executive summary ready to go, and that executive summary is why you are placing this call to this person at this time.

Another point while we're on this communications thing: always speak in terms that your customer can understand and relate to.

A decade ago, I was consulting with a company that was, for the first time, globalizing its operation. Up to that point, the divisions for each individual country pretty much did their own thing as long as it was along the general lines of dermatology. Make what you want to, market it how you want to, price it how you want to, just be sure to send your profits to headquarters. The countries were the individual fiefdoms of their operational presidents.

During the strategic planning session we conducted with the leadership team, it became pretty apparent this probably wasn't the most efficient way to conduct business. So the decision was made to develop a common operating process for all functional areas where it made sense to standardize. One of those areas was the IT system.

That led to a team being created whose mission was to prioritize all proposed IT projects. To include the entire company, this led to some teleconferences hooking up the IT folks from around the globe. Not surprisingly, English was not the native tongue for a number of the folks on the telecons.

With the company culture up to that point having been a Wild West operating environment, you can imagine the raging debates that were sparked as individual countries recoiled in shock as their pet projects were at first challenged and then, for the most part, eliminated. The process continued on to a project proposed by the US home office. Everyone else around the globe, having been told *no no no* on their own pet projects, was all too ready to pile on and give a thumbs down.

We all know that not all votes in the corporate world are equal, and this project was sponsored by the global VP of IT. After much raucous debate, he learned forward in his seat to be closer to the microphone and most emphatically stated to everyone on the telecon, "Look, this project impacts the entire company. We have no choice but to execute this one. End of discussion."

It was three weeks before Singapore figured out that "execute" actually meant "do the project." While the rest of the Company was busy implementing, they had deleted all funding and resources for the effort. Always speak in terms your customer can relate to.

These same techniques carry over to e-mail. We all get these rambling e-mail messes, and you know it as well as I do—as soon as someone has that reputation, you do not even bother to read those e-mails. We will not even deal with inappropriate things being passed around the Internet that you need to delete and get off your device immediately. As a little corporation like Microsoft can attest, your voicemail is not admissible in court but your e-mail is (United States vs. Microsoft (2001)). Anything that's on your computer can be used by your company to your detriment should it desire to do so.

Your e-mails should be exactly like your voicemails: bullet-pointed, clipped statements that are short and to the point, stating who is going to do what by when. If you have an attachment to put with it, that is just fine, but do not put tons of verbiage in the e-mail. If you are writing more than a single window that your e-mail screen will hold, you probably should think about sending an attachment that contains the pertinent information as opposed to this extensive novel that you are getting ready to broadcast to the world, telling everyone who sees it that you cannot prioritize nor state anything succinctly.

*Paying attention to simple little things that most people neglect makes a few people rich.—Henry Ford.*

# Conclusion

Well gang, that's about it. Now get out there and take control, remembering to do the following:

- Read the eyes! Proactively engage the audience with questions, and you'll know who's with you and who's not.
- Quantify your value proposition in terms customers use to manage their business. You can never go far wrong if that is in dollars.
- Seize that business environment! You'll get high marks for being different. Alas, it can mean more time to get ready, but as you already know, this should be no big deal. It's only your career.
- When challenged, run the LAER model. Read the eyes and go to your supporters. Break the communications cycle with the mortal enemy.
- To conclude the meeting, go to that flip chart and start describing the world exactly the way you want it to be, resulting in approval of your proposal/project. If the audience says nothing, you've got your post-meeting e-mail already crafted, with information on who will do what by when. More than likely, someone will say, "Wait a minute." But that is a good thing, not a bad thing. You now know what objection you must overcome to gain support for your plan. When that happens, merely return to concisely

stating your value proposition. Force that decision right now, when you have the maximum opportunity to impact it.

- Who would *you* want to do business with anyway?

Life is too short not to have some fun with it. And so I salute you and say, May you always find business success, and may your competition always know it. CARPEI AUDIENTIAM!

*"Now go do ... that voodoo ... that YOU do ... SO WELL!"*
—*Harvey Korman as Hedly Lamarr in Blazing Saddles*